MORTGAGE LOANS: WHAT'S RIGHT FOR YOU?

Second Edition

BY JAMES E. BRIDGES
with DEBORAH J. BRIDGES

Betterway Publications, Inc.
White Hall, Virginia

Published by Betterway Publications, Inc.
Post Office Box 219
Crozet, VA 22932
Telephone: (804) 823-5661

Cover design by Julienne McNeer
Typography by Typecasting

Copyright © 1986, 1989 by James E. Bridges

Library of Congress Cataloging-in-Publication Data

Bridges, James E.
    Mortgage loans.

    Includes index.
    1. Mortgage loans—United States. I. Bridges, Deborah J.
II. Title.
HG2040.5.U5B75   1989   332.7'22   89–14907
ISBN 1-55870-138-9 (pbk.)

Printed in the United States of America

0 9 8 7 6 5 4

Dedication

I believe that credit should be given where credit is due. This book was written at the prompting of my wife and, together with her hard work, it has been completed. Because of her deep concern for people, she wanted this book to be both informative and helpful. She has taken run-on sentences, incomplete thoughts, under- and oversimplifications, tricky jargon along with terms and phrases that would be foreign to anyone who is not familiar with financing and real estate, and turned them into an understandable book for the layperson.

I personally feel she has done 90% of the work. For this reason she appears as co-author of the book. In this way she will receive at least 50% of the credit for a job well done.

> *With love to my wife, Deborah Jane Bridges,*
> *Who is also my chief editor and staff.*
>
> *James E. Bridges*

Acknowledgments

We would like to thank the following people for their time and assistance and for contributing supportive information.

Mrs. Edythe C. Bridges, my mother; Douglas A. Baker, mortgage banker; L. Scott Watson, bank president; David Cunningham, mortgage insurer; John C. Bridges, my brother, builder and real estate broker; James Garrett, builder and land surveyor; Richard H. Johnston, attorney; Joseph M. Seidel; Kenny Davidson, loan officer; Clifford H. Holcombe, FmHA County Supervisor; Judy Dixon, FmHA, Office Clerk; Tom Buffton, V.A. Assistant Loan Guaranty Officer; Edward L. McNally, V.A. Chief Construction and Valuation Section; W.H. Roday, V.A. Chief Loan Officer, Service and Claims Section of the Atlanta Regional Office.

No acknowledgment would be complete without our giving thanks to God, who has helped us so greatly in the completion of this work and who gives so generously to us all.

Contents

Introduction

Mortgage Loans—What's Right For You? is designed to disclose the advantages and disadvantages of different financing programs, so that you can see for yourself which program is best suited for you. This book gives you enough knowledge to safeguard yourself. The potential home buyer need not be intimidated by the mortgage loan process. When viewed like any other purchase—using the same tools of information, interpretation, inspection, and selection—the consumer can rest assured that the best choice has been made.

First, put aside anything you know or have been told about home financing. In this manner, your mind can be creative to make your way through what seems like a maze and begin to simplify it. Viewing the maze of home financing is like viewing a jigsaw puzzle. Not knowing what the finished picture looks like, with only the pieces before you, you may be confused as to where to start. This book shows the entire picture, taking out each piece, one at a time, examining it in relationship to the whole and then replacing it, so that the complete picture is always before you. The picture here is home financing. The pieces are: sources of money, different types of loans, differences in these loans, the total loan package, advantages versus disadvantages, and qualifications.

This book may open your eyes to questions such as: Is this house suited to my needs? Did I apply for the right loan? With the right bank or mortgage company? Do I have to pay all the charges? Who else can pay? Am I getting a good deal? You need to understand completely what may be available in mortgage loans, as well as all of the loan terminology that defines and explains what is available, in order to make the best decision.

The process of buying a house consists of three principal stages:

☐ Finding and negotiating the purchase of the house. This includes writing the contract which states the price and terms of the sale.

☐ Acquiring the loan. This involves going to the bank or mortgage company and filling out an application. Your income and credit will be checked. The house will be appraised to determine its value. The loan is approved at this time.

☐ Closing the sale. This is the completion of the home buying process. A date will be set, called the "closing date." On this day you are entitled to take possession of the house. One or more lawyers normally handle the closing.

The first four chapters of this book deal with gaining an understanding of money, loans, terms, and the integration of all three. The next four chapters explain the costs of different items and the parts they play in the mortgage loan. Following those chapters the reader will find more beneficial explanations and options. By the time you reach chapter twelve you should be prepared to use the knowledge gained from the earlier chapters to make some decisions on the best loan for you. Chapter 13 will help you avoid home investment / mortgage traps, deals that rarely—if ever—are in your best interest.

Each chapter in *Mortgage Loans* is a piece of the puzzle. By acquiring a step-by-step understanding of each piece, you acquire a clear view— or understanding—of the entire puzzle. Just as a person who is a skilled chess player can take advantage of the knowledge he has of each piece on the board, the mortgage buyer can apply knowledge gained from this book.

This book has been written to be the most complete mortgage loan guide and handbook possible. However, it does not—cannot—answer all the questions concerning every specific loan and circumstance. It should give you the knowledge and understanding to ask the right questions of the right people if the answer is not provided in these pages. However, don't be surprised if you get different answers to the very same question. This means only that further research is in order. All the variables involved in home financing can be understood. If you read this book and apply what you have learned, you could save thousands of dollars over the lifetime of your mortgage.

1

Statement on Mortgage Loans

BASICALLY ALL THE SAME

In actuality there is only one type of home loan: one that you must pay back, as the word "loan" implies. From this point on, everything else is just a creative way of packaging a loan to produce a particular result. Certain ways of packaging may make the initial loan payments attractive to you, but the long term consequences of the loan could be disastrous. If something is given to you with one hand it is usually taken away with the other. A prime example is a car loan. Let's say you see an ad in the paper for a new car with an interest rate at below the market. You had looked at the car a week before and were quoted a price. Now upon return you are informed that price is not good at the new interest rate simply because the packaging has changed. The difference between the price you were quoted initially and the new price is being used to pay the bank for the amount that they would have earned with a higher interest rate. Something was given but something was also taken away.

A NEW WAY TO VIEW MONEY

Don't think of money as money but as anything else you would buy or sell, for example apples or bananas. In the business sectors of the world, money is bought and sold daily. What anyone is willing to pay in interest is what money is worth. Banks buy money and pay interest on it, for example, with your checking or savings account. The banks in turn "sell" the money to someone by lending it out with interest. The bank makes or loses money based on the difference between what they pay out in interest and what they receive in interest. So money should be viewed like any commodity, such as apples or bananas. When weather conditions prove harsh, a shortage of produce occurs and the price goes up based on supply and demand. Similarly, if money is in short supply and demand is good, that is, a lot of people are borrowing, the interest rate for money goes up based on supply and demand. Remember, money grows by interest, and interest creates money for someone.

SOURCES OF MORTGAGE MONEY

The most used sources of mortgage money for home loans are commercial banks, savings and loan associations, and mortgage companies. Mortgage loans are either government or non-government backed. Currently, government backed loans are one of the largest sources of mortgages. If a loan has any government backing or guarantee associated with it, then the loan is called a "government loan." Any other type loan usually is referred to as a "conventional loan." The money for home loans comes from depositors, sales of stocks and bonds, and insurance companies investing in mortgages. A separate book could be written on the selling of stocks and bonds (securities) for mortgage money so that issue will not be addressed in these pages.

Even if you are looking at a federal, state, or county bond program for home loans, those loans still are processed by "mortgage bankers." One good thing to keep in mind concerning state, county—and sometimes federal—home loan programs is that they usually are below long term market interest rates.

THE MORTGAGE LOAN PROCEDURE— SIMPLIFIED

When you first decide to purchase a home, an income or mortgage ratio can give you an estimate of the price house you can afford. Basically, this formula is 25% of your gross income per paycheck to be used towards a house payment. Using this formula you can begin to "househunt" and stay within a price range suitable to you. There may be some variances but the formula is a good basic guideline. A second formula that also is useful is 2½ to 3½ times your annual gross income calculated for the amount of a mortgage. The biggest problem with these formulas is that they do not consider interest rate or the type of loan you might obtain. Nevertheless, they do provide useful guidelines.

Generally, it is not until you are close to a decision on your house selection that you begin to search out financial options. However, the best time to consider financial options is *before* your selection, because the right type mortgage can mean so much when choosing the best house for your needs. Bank officers and mortgage representatives are in the business of making loans. It is to their advantage to be as friendly and helpful as possible, hoping that you will return to them to place your loan.

Many real estate agencies have mortgage people with whom they have dealt for years. You will be encouraged to use these people. Should they meet your needs, fine. If not, let both the real estate agency and the mortgage representative know that you want to place your loan elsewhere. There are numerous variables on mortgage loans. While most of them are standard, tailor-made loans sometimes are available to the financially qualified buyer. Normally loans run from 15 to 30 years with virtually no mortgage limit to the buyer who is qualified.

In general the loan process is preset from the time you find the house you want to purchase. Most agencies have other agencies with whom they work; like the real estate company having a "favorite" mortgage representative and the mortgage representative working with a P.M.I. (Private Mortgage Insurance) company and using a certain closing lawyer. Closing costs for a loan are thoroughly discussed in a chapter devoted totally to understanding these expenses better.

In most cases there are no set rules as to who may pay certain items related to the loan. In a buyer's market, when more houses are available than are being sold, the builder or seller may be willing to contribute to the sale's closing costs. In a seller's market, where he has more buyers than homes to sell, he does not need to give a buyer incentives. Once you have found a home that you like, the loan process begins. The next person that you will come in contact with will be the mortgage company's representative, or the bank's loan officer.

In terms of your personal involvement, the initial loan package can be "set up" in about an hour. The waiting game for approval is another story entirely. Unless there is a problem with your credit report you probably will have only one other meeting—to sign the completed paperwork. If you are even starting to think about buying a house in the future, and your credit rating is not what you would like it to be, begin now to clean up your credit. Make a couple of installment payments ahead of schedule or pay one off altogether. Pay down the balance on your charge cards. Make sure you are current on all your monthly accounts. The loan process will flow much more freely if your credit report is unencumbered by negative references.

The exact sequence of events for a loan application may differ, depending on all the circumstances involved. The attorneys used for the closing represent the mortgage company or bank making the loan and not the purchaser. In some cases you have a choice of attorneys to use and in others you do not. Laws governing mortgage loans will affect certain procedures. The amount of time it takes to get a mortgage loan may vary according to the type and amount loan and the volume of business being handled by the bank or mortgage company at the time of your application.

RESPA EXPLAINED

RESPA stands for the Real Estate Settlement Procedures Act of 1974. It became effective on June 30, 1976. The law requires that after a written loan application has been submitted, the lender must provide you with a good faith estimate of the cost involved and a copy of the *Settlement Cost* booklet. This information is given when the loan application is taken or mailed within three business days. This law does not set the charges of the mortgage bankers but rather requires that they disclose all the charges as a good faith estimate so the home buyer can make an informed decision. The settlement costs booklet explains the home buyer's rights and obligations. There is a wealth of information in this book to benefit the potential home buyer. The RESPA law is for consumer protection against unfair practices in matters related to real estate transactions and the disclosure of charges. Many times when government tries to regulate something there is also a loss to the public. Such is the case with the RESPA. Mortgage bankers are limited, by law, as to what they can say or do to help the potential home buyer. This matter is discussed further in chapter twelve under "Your Qualifications."

Another subject controlled by law is the rights of the home owner who is overdue on his house payments. How late and how far behind a person may get on the payments depends on the agreements that were signed and by prevailing state law. If the loan is a government-backed loan, the federal law will override the state law. All states, however, do not have the same laws governing mortgage loans, refinancing, and second mortgages.

2

Who Is Fannie Mae? Freddy Mac? Ginnie Mae?

This chapter will deal mainly with government-related loans. Fannie Mae, Freddy Mac and Ginnie Mae are all sources of government secured and/or insured mortgages. They are just another piece of the puzzle of mortgage loans.

Fannie Mae stands for Federal National Mortgage Association and deals in Federal Housing Administration (F.H.A.) and Veterans Administration (V.A.) loans and also conventional loans. Freddie Mac is the Federal Home Loan Mortgage Corporation and is concerned with conventional loans. Ginnie Mae is the Government National Mortgage Association dealing with F.H.A. and V.A. loans. These agencies do not deal directly with the public but do business through approved mortgage companies (mortgage bankers). The money for these loans does not come from government sources; however, it comes from private sources, mainly the sale of securities.

The Balanced Budget and Emergency Deficit Reduction Law of 1985, better known as the *Gramm-Rudman Law*, requires the elimination of deficit spending by our government by 1991. No business could have survived having been mismanaged the way our government has been. It is time for a change, but this change cannot come without sacrifices. Some of those changes are going to affect the mortgage loan programs. Some programs may be completely eliminated or severely cut back. They may run short of funds and be forced to make temporary cutbacks in their services. This may mean that the mortgage monies available at the beginning of a year will not be available at the end of the year. When Congress and the President prepare the budget for a fiscal year, certain loan programs could be cut back or eliminated altogether.

This will be an ever changing process until stability in revenue and spending is achieved. For this reason, when you shop for a mortgage loan ask questions to determine if the program is suspected of being cut back or eliminated. Until 1991 it looks as if "anything goes." For example, *H.U.D.* (Housing and Urban Development) is studying a way to sell F.H.A. Although this book endeavors to be as accurate and current as possible, the market is ever-changing and you should examine carefully any loan program you are considering, particularly any government loan program.

V.A. ADVANTAGES

V.A. stands for the Veterans Administration. The Administration guarantees the home loans of some veterans but it does not lend the money. V.A. does not guarantee a loan per se to the veteran but rather guarantees repayment to the private mortgage company. The V.A. puts up the money for the loan should the veteran default (foreclose).

Anyone who has served in the U.S. Armed Forces is a veteran. But not all veterans are eligible for a V.A. loan. Eligibility depends upon the length of time served and the law that governed the veteran at the time of his/her service. Different laws govern the eligibility of a veteran. Depending upon the law, required active duty time may vary. Peacetime service is from 181 days to 2 years to qualify but a veteran of wartime service can begin to qualify with as little as 90 days of service. In the event of an in-service injury, the veteran may have special eligibility privileges. The laws governing veterans' eligibility for V.A. mortgage loans will not be covered in this book because there are too many variables to be considered. An example of the complexity of V.A. eligibility is the *Veterans Administration pamphlet 26–4* description of other types of service:

☐ Certain United States citizens who serviced in the armed forces of a government allied with the United States in World War II

☐ Unmarried surviving spouses of the above-described persons who died as the result of service or service-connected injuries. (Children of deceased veterans are not eligible.)

☐ The spouse of any member of the Armed Forces serving on active duty who is listed as missing in action, or is a prisoner of war and has been so listed for a total of more than 90 days.

☐ Individuals with service as members in certain other organizations, services, programs and schools may also be eligible. Questions about whether this service qualifies for home loan benefits should be referred to the Loan Guaranty Division of the nearest V.A. regional office.

There have been cases where a veteran was eligible for a loan guarantee but did not know it. A veteran could be missing out on a loan guarantee either because of misunderstanding or lack of knowledge. For these reasons, veterans should contact the nearest V.A. office to find out their eligibility.

Remember, the V.A. office is there to help and assist the veteran. Those working at the V.A. have the best interest of the veterans at heart and truly try to help them. However, this book will cover some facts on V.A. loans and basic eligibility.

To be eligible for a V.A. loan a veteran must have an honorable discharge. The exception to this is an "inservice loan," when the veteran is still on active duty. If, in the line of duty, a serviceman is killed, then the spouse may qualify for V.A. eligibility if the spouse has not remarried. There are no age restrictions on veterans, meaning that even a veteran sixty (60) years of age could get a thirty (30) year loan. Any home purchased under V.A. guidelines must be occupied by the veteran or the spouse of an active-duty service member. The spouse's eligibility to satisfy the occupancy requirement is a recent change and applies to loans made after January 21, 1988. "The property must be located in the United States, its territories, or possessions. The latter consist of Puerto Rico, Guam, Virgin Islands, American Samoa and Northern Mariana Islands." (VA Pamphlet 26-4)

For a veteran to obtain a V.A. loan he must meet V.A. requirements (underwriting standards of the Veterans Administration). Underwriting standards are things like income guidelines pertaining to the ratio of monthly income to monthly mortgage payments, as well as total monthly obligations and credit worthiness. To quote V.A. Pamphlet 26-4 once again, "You must have enough income to meet the new mortgage payment on the loan, cover the cost of owning a home, take care of other obligations and expenses and still have enough income left over for family support (a spouse's income is considered in the same manner as the veteran's)."

A veteran needs his DD214 when talking to the V.A. Eligibility is determined from the DD214 and a certificate of eligibility is issued if qualified. If the original copy has been lost, the veteran can obtain a copy of the DD214 by writing the branch of military service served. Even if it has been years since discharge, the amount of the eligibility is now the same for all veterans. There are certain stipulations under which a veteran may use his eligibility more than once. Currently, when the first V.A. mortgage loan is paid off, the veteran's eligibility is reinstated; however, there are stipulations that apply. The Property Rehabilitation Act of 1987 (Pub. L. 100-198) states that eligibility may not be restored under certain conditions. It is highly recommended that veterans contact their nearest V.A. office for specifics.

Full V.A. eligibility at present is $36,000. Don't be confused with the veteran's eligibility amount and the amount of the home loan. The veteran's eligibility amount is usually the amount that the V.A. will insure payment by the veteran to the mortgage lender. This is the lender's security in case of the veteran's foreclosure. Loan limits are raised from time to time, and when this takes place the limits are applicable to all veterans even if the veteran has previously used his eligibility.

The Veteran's Administration has no standard requirement on the maximum amount of a loan that it will guarantee to a qualified veteran (25% to 50% average). V.A. guarantees to the mortgage banker a percentage of the loan. For example, a veteran wants to buy a $75,000 house but his eligibility is $25,000. The $25,000 is the amount that will be insured by the administration. For this reason mortgage lenders have their own V.A. requirements, not to be confused with those of the administration. Lenders do this in order to safeguard themselves against veteran loan default. V.A. loans can be "shopped" for like any other home loan, meaning that if one lender cannot make a particular size loan another may.

A qualified veteran can obtain a 100% guaranteed loan. Presently the Government National Mortgage Association (Ginnie Mae) limits the amount of a no-down payment loan to four times the guaranty amount. This would be a guarantee that is equal to the sales price or appraised value, whichever is less; in other words, no down payment would be required. So, it is easy to understand all the confusion about the size of the loan and the amount of the veteran's eligibility. The following example may clarify loan amounts and veteran's eligibility:

A veteran with $36,000 eligibility wants a 100% loan to buy a house with a sales price of $125,000. Remember, the mortgage company may allow the qualified veteran to obtain a loan that is four times his eligibility. Four times $36,000 is $144,000, so the veteran on this loan is eligible for a 100% loan.

However, had the sales price of the house been $150,000, the veteran would need a down payment. Down payments are calculated at 25% of the difference, making the down payment in this example 25% of $6,000, or $1,500. Conventional loans could easily be 10% of the sales price which would be $15,000. The benefits of a V.A. loan become evident.

When a veteran wishes to sell the house that he purchased with a V.A. loan, he must first notify the mortgage company that made the loan. Depending upon the company's option, the loan may be assumed or may become immediately due and payable; the determining factor in this situation is the credit of the purchaser. If the new buyer has good credit the veteran may be released from the liability to the V.A. This change was implemented on all loans that V.A. guaranteed on or after March 1, 1988.

In the event that a veteran needs an extension of his loan which would reduce the amount of monthly payments but, of course, extend the life of the loan, the amount that can be refinanced is now limited to 90% of the appraised value of the house. This limitation took effect February 20, 1988. Refinancing, which allows the old loan to be calculated with a new lower interest rate, is not affected by the new limitation.

Remember that any raise by Congress in the veterans' eligibility would raise the amount of 100% loans, therefore benefiting the veterans, by raising the V.A. guaranty. Furthermore, if the husband and wife are eligible veterans they may pool their amounts and increase their guaranty entitlement. Although the veteran may have obtained a 100% loan he may still need money, at closing, for other things such as closing costs and prepaid items. These additional money items are discussed in the chapter under closing costs and prepaids.

If for any reason a veteran's loan is foreclosed and V.A. has to pay a claim, V.A. will go after the veteran for the amount of the claim. V.A. has many options to collect this claim amount. Remember, V.A. is a federal agency with federal laws governing it. Federal law, in this case, will override state law. V.A. does not need a deficiency judgment to collect. It is best to talk with V.A. before going to a mortgage company for a V.A. loan, to know all the facts concerning your rights and obligations under this program.

The advantages of the V.A. guaranteed mortgage loan are: the qualified veteran can obtain a 100% loan; the mortgage loan is fully assumable, non-escalating (if closed prior to March 1, 1988), non-qualifying, with no prepayment penalties; it allows for refinancing, protection from quick foreclosure, guarantee of a mortgage loan at no cost to the veteran. These advantages will become clearer in the following chapter. A qualified veteran can purchase a home for one dollar ($1.00) which includes all prepaids and closing costs, if he is dealing with a willing seller. The exception to the "$1.00 move in" for the veteran concerns manufactured homes (e.g., grounded trailers and mobile homes). These types of homes require a 5% down payment, effective February 1, 1988. How to do this is covered in chapter twelve.

The main disadvantage of a V.A. guaranteed mortgage loan is that upon foreclosure, when the V.A. must pay a claim, the administration will seek recovery directly from the veteran.

Keep in mind that, for the qualified veteran, V.A. is the best mortgage program available. The Veterans Administration is extremely sensitive to the veteran's needs and will try to lean in favor of the veteran. The V.A. was established so that the veteran could compete with other buyers, who had good jobs and down payment money, thus making the veteran a competitive buyer.

F.H.A. BENEFITS

F.H.A. stands for the Federal Housing Administration, a department of Housing and Urban Development (H.U.D.). Anyone can obtain an F.H.A. loan guaranty provided the guidelines and requirements are met. Permanent residency but not citizenship is an F.H.A. requirement. An F.H.A. guaranteed mortgage loan requires less down payment than a conventional loan. Just like a V.A. loan, F.H.A. does not make the loan but rather guarantees the loan to the lender. The difference between the two is that F.H.A. guarantees the mortgage lender 100% of the loan, upon foreclosure. This guaranty is at a cost to the borrower and is called mortgage insurance, whereas a veteran has no extra cost to him at this time.

At the present time the money for a minimum down payment on an F.H.A. loan is computed at 3% of the first $25,000 and 5% thereafter until F.H.A.'s maximum loan amount is reached. A house with a price of $75,000 would be figured at 3% of $25,000 ($750) and 5% of $50,000 ($2500) making the total down payment being $3250. Additional monies are needed at the closing besides the down payment. These are called prepaid items, and are discussed in chapter eight.

There are exceptions to the 3% of the first $25,000 rule. First, when the selling price of the home does not exceed $50,000, the down payment is figured at 3% of the selling price. Another exception is when F.H.A. makes a combination loan to a veteran, who has at least 90 days to 2 years of active duty, and a certificate of veteran's status from V.A. to give to the mortgage company applying to F.H.A. for the veteran's loan. (Do not confuse the certificate of eligibility with the certificate of veteran's status. They are two entirely different documents.) The certificate of veteran's status enables a veteran to get the first $25,000 without a down payment but the remainder, thereafter, is figured at 5% until F.H.A.'s maximum loan amount is reached.

F.H.A. has no age limits for loan applicants for up to a thirty (30) year loan. Someone who has reached sixty (60) years of age or older may borrow the money for the down payment and prepaid items from a company, corporation or individual approved by H.U.D. These sources cannot have any involvement whatsoever with the sale of the home.

F.H.A. has many types of loans which will be discussed in the next chapter. Maximum loan amounts vary. F.H.A. has a standard mortgage limit and a high cost area mortgage limit. Depending upon the location of the house, state, county, etc., F.H.A. will determine the maximum amount of the loan by these guidelines.

The benefits of an F.H.A. loan guaranty are: a lower down payment than conventional loan, the loans are fully assumable, non-escalating, non-qualifying and require no prepayment penalties. F.H.A.'s purpose is to provide mortgage insurance (guaranteed loans) to lenders so that the lenders will be inclined to make loans to the first time home buyer. However, F.H.A. programs are not limited to the first time home buyer.

Loan assumptions made after December 1, 1986 contain a provision requiring the buyer to be found credit-worthy if the contract of sale is executed less than 24 months after execution of the mortgage or less than 24 months after a prior transfer of the property. Effective October 1, 1986 lenders are required to report all foreclosures to a national credit reporting bureau (NAHB).

REQUIREMENTS: YOU AND YOURS

Any mortgage loan approval is a two-step process. First, the property must be appraised and, second, the borrower must be approved. There are requirements for the house as well as requirements for the borrower. Mortgage companies handle loan processing. Basically, the mortgage company is a "go-between." They deal directly with the agencies, e.g. F.H.A., V.A. and lenders involved in the loan.

Any source of mortgage money has guidelines or requirements for the borrower such as: minimum amount of down payment (a percentage of the loan), maximum loan amounts, monthly income compared to total housing cost, monthly income to total monthly obligations, credit worthiness and job stability or security.

All sources of mortgage money require appraisals. The appraisals must be done by an appraiser who is qualified and approved by the lender and/or agency. An appraisal is required to assure the lender that the property is worth the sale's price and that the required loan to value ratio is met. An appraisal is supposed to represent a reasonable estimate of value and is based on comparable sales in the area. An appraisal is a lengthy document and in most cases what the buyer sees is the result of the appraisal rather than the actual appraisal. This short version of an appraisal is referred to as a C.r.V., certificate of reasonable value. Appraisals are good for only a specified length of time. These appraisals establish a reasonable estimate of value, insuring that a house is not overpriced for the area and that the lending institute does not over lend.

F.H.A. and V.A. appraisals, on existing homes, are presently good for six months. F.H.A. and V.A. appraisals on new construction are good for nine to twelve months. An F.H.A. appraisal adds closing costs to the appraisal and these costs are financed in with the loan. F.H.A. and V.A. require a warranty on new construction less than one year old. No warranty is required on existing homes. When F.H.A. appraises and accepts a house for a loan, it issues a "conditional commitment" to the mortgage company. The conditional commitment only obligates H.U.D. to insure a mortgage if a qualified borrower is found. F.H.A. will accept a V.A. appraisal and convert it to F.H.A. and add closing costs provided that the appraisal is not over nine months old. V.A. will accept an F.H.A. appraisal and deduct closing costs from the appraisal. Appraisals can be transferred or assigned from one mortgage company to another. A buyer does have the option to go with whatever approved mortgage company he chooses. He is not obligated to stay with the company that has made the appraisal.

Conventional appraisals, which are appraisals on all loans that do not have government backing, may have different time limits but most are good for six months. There are no required warranties on conventional loans. New construction, as well as existing, carries no required warranty with a conventional loan. Conventional appraisals are not interchangeable with F.H.A. or V.A. appraisals. However, conventional appraisals may be transferred. The validity of a transfer is solely at the discretion of the mortgage companies.

A buyer can pay more or less than the appraised value. If the buyer pays more than the appraised value, he must pay the difference in cash. If the buyer pays less than the appraised value, the loan amount is based on sales price.

All appraisals will list any serious and obvious defects on the appraisal form. These defects refer to structural problems rather than cosmetic, but judgment is left up to the appraiser. Any defects have to be corrected for the house to qualify for the loan. The seller should pay for the cost of repairs because an appraisal is given with the value of the repairs having been done. If a house needed a new roof, had the kitchen tile peeling up and carpet badly worn, this work would have to be done before the loan could be closed. Existing houses are generally sold "as is." Unless the repairs are listed on the appraisal, there would be no required repairs. The only exception to this would be a written agreement in the contract between buyer and seller to have such repairs done. Some real estate companies do offer a one year service warranty at a reasonable price to the buyer on new and existing homes. Because of the "as is" status on existing houses, the home buyer should carefully examine the house and seek professional advice if the situation warrants it, especially if the buyer is unsure.

F.H.A. and V.A. require warranties on new construction but the agencies will accept other warranties, e.g. H.O.W. (Home Owners Warranty), or Home Buyers warranty. These warranties are, primarily, extended structural warranties. Builders who offer these warranties must be approved by F.H.A. and V.A. and the companies that offer the warranties. F.H.A. and V.A. warranties are like their loans; neither actually warrants a house but rather each provides a warranty for the protection of the home buyer. Should there be a dispute, F.H.A. and V.A. will be a liaison but will not litigate in a matter. The buyer is still obligated to continue payments. No dispute releases him from this obligation. A new home, less than a year old, not built under F.H.A., may be eligible for a F.H.A. loan. In that case, the loan would be a *low ratio home loan* and would have no warranty. However, this loan would require a larger down payment than ordinary F.H.A. loans. A new home, less than one year old, but not built under F.H.A. specifications, can qualify for a V.A. loan if plans and specifications are certified by the builder and are submitted as evidence to insure that the house meets V.A. minimum property requirements. (F.H.A. and V.A. used the M.P.S. or minimum property standards up until December 1985. Now F.H.A. and V.A. require that the house meet city, county and/or state codes and minimum property requirements which are still in effect.)

Conventional loans normally require 5 to 10 percent down payment. The purchaser or seller can pay closing costs and discount points, an amount charged for balancing the loan's interest rate to current market yields, but the purchaser must pay prepaid items. F.H.A. will allow either party to pay the closing costs and discount points but again the purchaser must pay the prepaid items. At present, an F.H.A. loan cannot contribute more than six percent (6%) of the mortgage amount towards discount points and/or closing costs. The buyer must pay all costs above the 6% figure. This percentage is always subject to change.

V.A. will not allow the veteran to pay discounts but either party can pay the closing costs and prepaid items. V.A. charges a one percent funding fee and either party can pay it. These charges and costs will be discussed further in other chapters. Not all mortgage companies deal in all of the programs that V.A. and F.H.A. offer. If you are unable to find a mortgage company to work with you or if you do not know whether a particular program is still in effect, contact the V.A./F.H.A. office nearest you for information.

THE RULE TO REMEMBER

The buyer must meet certain guidelines and requirements on mortgage loans. If credit problems have occurred in the past, full disclosure is the best means of getting assistance. Reasonable explanations are a valuable tool to the loan representative, who works on behalf of the buyer. Even someone who has had hard times, perhaps a bankruptcy or foreclosure, has been able to purchase a home after re-establishing his credit. So the rule to remember is be honest and open when needing help.

3

Loans Defined

In this chapter loans will be defined but the particular costs involved will not be discussed. Understanding the inner-workings of these loans is far more important than having a cost projection. Once the structure of loans is understood, the advantages and disadvantages are more easily grasped.

ADJUSTABLE OR ARM

The ARM (adjustable rate mortgage) offers an interest rate that is "adjustable" throughout the entire life of the loan, and payments change accordingly. A good ARM loan has "caps": restrictive measures that prevent the payments from increasing, thus protecting the buyer, or decreasing, thus protecting the mortgage company, beyond a predetermined maximum amount.

The Federal Reserve Board and the Federal Home Loan Bank Board define the adjustable rate mortgage or A.R.M. as one where the interest rate changes periodically and payments may go up or down. Lenders generally charge lower initial interest rates for ARMs than for fixed-rate mortgages. This makes the ARM easier on the pocketbook, at first, than a fixed-rate mortgage for the same loan amount. It also means that you might qualify for a larger loan because lenders sometimes make this decision on the basis of your current income and the first and/or second year's payments. Moreover, your ARM could be less expensive over a long period of time than a fixed-rate mortgage, for example, if interest rates remain steady or decrease.

Against these advantages, the home buyer must weigh the risk that an increase in interest rates would lead to higher monthly payments in the future. It's a trade-off, getting a lower rate with an ARM in exchange for assuming more risk.

There are many different ARM programs. At present F.H.A. and most mortgage companies offer an ARM loan. The V.A. doesn't offer ARM loans, nor are ARM loans currently available on the biweekly payment program (defined in subsequent paragraphs). These loans may differ considerably. It is vitally important that the buyer be aware of what the highest monthly payment could possibly be, over the entire life of the loan, and make his judgment, for or against an ARM loan, with this criteria rather than using the lowest current payment as a scale. An amendment to the Truth-in-Lending (Regulation 2) of the Federal Reserve Board is proposed to require the credit contract to clearly specify the maximum interest rate that will accrue during the life of the loan.

ASSUMABLE

An assumable loan is actually more of a term within the confines of a loan agreement. Basically it is the right of one buyer to take over the mortgage loan obligations of another. In the original loan agreement, a stipulation(s) either gives or denies assumability of the loan.

BIWEEKLY

Biweekly mortgages, allowing homeowners to make their loan payments biweekly instead of monthly, and usually on the same schedule as their pay periods, save tens of thousands of dollars and offer automatic deduction on loan payments, thereby offering a more convenient alternative. The biweekly loan is for people who are very disciplined, and have enough cash that they can afford to make the payments every two weeks.

The advantages of a biweekly mortgage include fast equity buildup and shorter loan term, substantial interest savings, and affordable payments. All money from extra payments goes toward reducing the outstanding balance on a home loan. The pay-back period can be even faster: the higher the interest rate, the faster it will pay off if a biweekly mortgage is used. In addition, the higher the rate, the more saved in interest payments over the life of a biweekly loan.

Biweekly mortgages are used by lenders mainly to set themselves apart from their competition. Generally, lenders will not offer biweekly mortgages unless the borrower has an account with the same institution. The growing number of borrowers who travel a great deal will appreciate the convenience of automatic deduction. Automatic deduction of loan payments, common with biweeklies, virtually eliminates late payments.

Paying a mortgage biweekly is the equivalent of making 13 mortgage payments each year, which decreases the life of a 30-year mortgage to 18 to 22 years. Similar results can be achieved by homeowners who pay their mortgages monthly if they make a thirteenth payment, to be applied to the loan principal, at the end of each year. On a $100,000, 30-year fixed rate loan at 10 percent interest, a homeowner would save $67,155 over the life of the loan.

Many lending institutions are skeptical of the biweeklies because they don't believe there's a significant demand for the loans. However, the popularity of biweekly mortgages has increased with the February 1988 decision of the Federal National Mortgage Association (Fannie Mae) to purchase biweekly loans and sell them to investors on the secondary mortgage market. The agency has not only purchased and packaged about $115 million of biweekly loans since that decision, but it has standby commitments to purchase another $100 million.

Borrowers commonly have to pay a slightly higher interest rate than they would on a 30-year fixed rate loan, because biweeklies are more expensive loans to service. In addition, payments on a biweekly mortgage are five to eight percent higher than for a 30-year fixed rate loan. Most lenders won't allow a borrower with a conventional mortgage to switch to a biweekly loan payment. If they want the biweekly loan, they must refinance, pay new points, closing costs, and other fees associated with refinancing.

BUY DOWNS

This is a situation where the actual interest rate is lowered, temporarily or permanently, by the seller. He pays money to the mortgage company to lower the interest rate of the buyer. The interest for the buyer has changed but the interest to the mortgage company has not. The company still receives the original amount but it is paid by the seller. An example would be something called a "3–2–1 buy down," in the disguise of an ad that reads "9% interest." What may be taking place is that the seller is buying down the interest rate, 3% the first year, 2% the second year, 1% the third year and at the fourth year the interest rate returns to the original rate of the mortgage loan. Some lenders now have a limit on the amount that the seller can contribute to a buy down. There are different ways to structure a buy down and they can be used on many different loans.

Example: $60,000 loan @ 12% interest fixed rate
monthly payment = $617.40*
Seller buys down this monthly payment at a percentage rate of
3% the first year making the monthly payment = $483.00* (9% interest)
2% the second year " " " " = $526.80* (10% interest)
1% the third year " " " " = $571.80* (11% interest)
4th year the monthly payments = $617.40* (12% interest)
   *Payment is principal and interest on $60,000 amortized for 30 years

**CONFORMING/
NON-CONFORMING**

A conforming loan meets the stipulations of the lending institution. A non-conforming loan does not meet those stipulations. Take for example a sales price of a home at $95,000. If the buyer wants an F.H.A. loan, he will have to pay a down payment of $4,250 (3% of the 1st $25,000 = $750, 5% of the balance of $70,000 = $3,500). That down payment reduces the loan amount to $90,750. But say the maximum F.H.A. loan amount available was $85,250. To make this a conforming loan the buyer would have to put down an additional $5,500

($90,750 − $85,250 = $5,500) or F.H.A. would not make (guarantee) the loan. The buyer's option would be to make the additional down payment or seek another source with higher loan limits. Another source might handle *jumbo* loans, which have higher loan amounts than normal, starting around $168,700. Jumbo loans start where Fannie Mae and Freddy Mac loans top out which is currently $168,700. However, some states such as Hawaii and California have even higher ceilings due to a higher cost of living scale.

No company makes a non-conforming loan but it is a term you will hear when a loan is unacceptable to the mortgage company. To summarize conforming/non-conforming loans, the former meets the lender's qualifications and the latter does not.

CONSTRUCTION PERMANENT/ ROLLOVER

This type of loan is infrequently used but has its own advantages. Generally, a construction loan is for a short period of time, usually not over one year, and then the builder must pay the bank the money that he borrowed to build the home. A permanent loan refers to any loan with a longer payback period, along the line of 15 to 30 years. Using a *Construction Permanent* loan there is only one closing for the land, construction and financing of the home. At this closing a date is set, so that after the construction phase, the loan converts to permanent loan for the buyer. The construction permanent, or C/P loan as it is sometimes called, would save the closing costs and fee that would occur at the permanent loan closing. Another name for this type loan is rollover because it converts and serves two purposes.

CONVERTIBLE/ CONVERSION

A provision to convert in a loan document provides an alternative to the original loan agreement. If the provision is used there may be additional charge. An example would be a provision to set the interest rate at a permanent percentage (or fixed rate) in years three through five of an adjustable loan, at the option of the buyer. Options or provisions would need to be exercised within the specified time limit or they become void. Many times the option to convert has stipulations such as payments having been made in a timely manner, etc.

ESCALATING/ NON-ESCALATING

These are terms rather than types of loans and are tied to the assumability of a mortgage loan agreement. An escalating clause is a stipulation that, upon sale, the interest rate may go up for the new buyer. There are no set escalating clauses. This matter is left up to the lender and the state law. The interest rate of the loan does not increase upon the sale of a home with an assumable loan agreement and a non-escalating clause. *Prepayment Penalty* is a clause whereby if the loan is paid off before a specified date or before term, a penalty is imposed that is usually a percentage of the loan balance. Some lenders will allow only a certain amount to be paid on the principal each year, above the amortization, without imposing a prepayment penalty.

FM.H.A. OR FARMERS HOME ADMINISTRATION

More commonly referred to as the Farmers Home Loan, FM.H.A. is a rural credit agency of the U.S. Department of Agriculture. This book will discuss only the residential single family home loan program of the Fm.H.A. These are 100% loans for a length of thirty-three years and must be in designated rural areas. The interest is subsidized, and can be as low as 1%. Upon the sale of the home the government can request a portion of the monies received to be returned to them for their participation in the low interest loan. This is called a *recapture provision*. Fm.H.A. has maximum house size, lot size, credit standards and minimum and maximum income requirements. Income requirements are based on number in family. The larger the family the more income a person could have and still qualify for the loan.

Fm.H.A. program is designed to be the place of last resort to obtain a loan. If a person can make the standard down payment and qualify for the loan through normal credit channels then they would not qualify under the Fm.H.A. program. This program serves a very useful, needed purpose and is for new as well as old homes. If a person thinks they might fit into Fm.H.A. requirements they would do well to check it out. The availability of these loans depends upon the money that Fm.H.A. has at the time. To obtain this loan a person does not go through a mortgage company but directly to the Fm.H.A. office.

To quote Fm.H.A. of U.S.D.A.

> Fm.H.A. loans make it possible for families of low and moderate income to become owners of adequate homes. When the financial position of the family improves so that the loan can be refinanced through a commercial lender, the loan contract provides that this shall be done.

> The applicant pays for the legal services necessary to guarantee a satisfactory title to the site, for credit reports, and other incidental loan closing costs. These expenses may be included in the loan.

> Applications may be made at the Farmers Home Administration county office serving the area in which the house is located.

> Anyone unable to locate the FmHA county office in the local telephone directory may write to the Farmers Home Administration, U.S. Department of Agriculture, Washington, D.C. 20250.

The Gramm–Rudman Law may cause many things to change temporarily or permanently. It is best to call the Farmers Home Administration county office about the guidelines or requirements pertaining to the program that interests you, for an update.

F.H.A.

The Federal Housing Administration or F.H.A. is a department of Housing and Urban Development, or H.U.D., which guarantees repayment of a loan should the buyer default. F.H.A. does not designate a particular type of loan. F.H.A. backs loans on single family dwellings such as single family detached, single family attached, e.g.

townhouses, condominiums, duplexes, triplexes and quadraplexes, and mobile homes. F.H.A. mortgage limits are presently at $67,500 for low cost areas and $101,350 for high cost. F.H.A. mortgages may be repaid in monthly payments over a term of 10, 15, 20, 25, and 30 years. Some of the F.H.A. mortgage insurance programs are:

1. Fixed rate mortgage payment
2. Adjustable rate (ARM) limited by Congress to the number that can be made each year
3. Graduated Payment (GPM)
   The GPM program is limited to owner-occupant and requires a larger down payment; in addition there are five plans under GPM:
   Section 245-A for new or existing home
   > Plan I monthly payments increase 2½% each year for five years
   > Plan II monthly payments increase 5% each year for five years
   > Plan III monthly payments increase 7½% each year for five years
   > Plan IV monthly payments increase 2% each year for ten years
   > Plan V monthly payments increase 3% each year for ten years
   It is best to talk with a mortgage company about any of these plans because they are continually being updated.
4. GEM or Growing Equity Mortgage (245a)—shorter mortgage terms saving interest cost
5. Mortgage Insurance for Disaster Victims (Section 203h)
   "This program provides mortgage insurance for loans financing the purchase of a one family dwelling by the victim of a disaster. In order to qualify, the home previously occupied must have been damaged or destroyed by a catastrophe and the area must have been designated by the President to be a major disaster area." (H.U.D.) The mortgage limit depends upon the area but no downpayment is required.
6. Rehabilitation (203k) program provides mortgage insurance on loans used to:
   1) rehabilitate an existing single family house
   2) to rehabilitate and refinance the outstanding indebtedness or
   3) to purchase and rehabilitate; this program may be used to convert a non-residential building to residential or change the number of family units in the building.
7. F.H.A./V.A.—a loan made by F.H.A for veterans with 90 days to 2 years active duty (refer to previous chapter under F.H.A.)
8. Service Members (Section 222)—Coast Guard and National Oceanic and Atmospheric Administration
9. Investor—Guidelines and requirements are different. A larger down payment is required.
10. Interest Subsidy (Section 235)—for low to moderate income home-buyers (No funds are available for this program at the present time. This program had restrictions on the minimum and maximum income; maximum cost of the house; government subsidy to the mortgage company to as low as 4%. If the program is re-funded the guidelines may also change.)
11. Home Improvement (Title I, Section 2)—loans to finance home improvements

The F.H.A. loans listed above are not the total number of different loans that are offered but they are the more commonly used programs. The previous chapter will be very helpful in understanding F.H.A.

The Gramm–Rudman Law may cause many things to change temporarily or permanently. It is best to call an approved mortgage company about the guidelines or requirements pertaining to the program that interests you, or call the F.H.A. office nearest you for an update.

FIXED RATE

This is a loan that has the same interest rate and mortgage payment for the term of the loan.

FIXED RATE 30 YEAR WITH 15 YEAR BALLOON

This is a loan that has the same interest rate with the same monthly payment computed on a 30 year payback with one very big exception. The entire loan is due and payable in full at the end of the 15th year. The buyer receives the payments of a thirty (30) year loan, thus keeping the payments down, but has only fifteen (15) years to pay. At that time the remainder, or loan balance, is due. This type loan could be structured or computed on a fixed rate loan for any number of years' payback, 15–20–30 years, etc. with a balloon payment placed at any given year, 5–10–15, etc. This type loan is used when the investor does not want to commit to a loan of a specific length of time; he wants an "out" option at the time of the balloon. The investor commits only to the years until the balloon. The loan may or may not have a provision to refinance at the time of the balloon. The advantage to this "time-bomb" loan is that the interest that is being paid is generally lower than the longer term mortgage. A buyer who has the funds to make the balloon payment would save thousands in interest but the buyer who does not is playing with dynamite.

G.E.M.

A rarely used loan, this stands for Growing Equity Mortgage. It is a graduated payment loan designed with scheduled increase in payments which are applied directly to principal reduction. As a result, GEMs have substantially shorter mortgage terms than typical mortgages. This shorter term dramatically reduces the interest cost on a mortgage.

GRADUATED PAYMENT

The payments on a graduated loan would always increase, say from year to year, until they reached a maximum amount. This is not to be confused with with an adjustable mortgage where the payments can go up or down. The payments always increase because unpaid interest is added back to the payment. A percentage of the interest payment is postponed, by a yearly predetermined amount, and added back to the loan balance. The advantages of this type loan would be tied to the circumstances of the individual. It would particularly benefit someone who expects a substantial rise in income over time.

An example, as it would be stated by a mortgage company:

(1) a 30 year graduated payment loan where
(2) true interest rate is 10¾%

(3) payments (not interest) increase at 7½% per year for five years

(4) payments remain the same beginning at the sixth year

Perhaps the following chart will help to further explain the graduated mortgage payment loan of a $68,800 vs. straight interest loans.

starting payment of $509.02   1st yr. payment

$509.02 \times 7.5\% = 38.18 + 509.02 = 547.20$ 2nd ″   ″

$547.20 \times 7.5\% = 41.04 + 547.20 = 588.24$ 3rd ″   ″

$588.24 \times 7.5\% = 44.12 + 588.24 = 632.36$ 4th ″   ″

$632.36 \times 7.5\% = 47.43 + 632.36 = 679.79$ 5th ″   ″

$679.79 \times 7.5\% = 50.98 + 679.79 = 730.77$ 6th thru 30th yr

$68,800 at 10¾% interest only (no principal paid off) payment of $616.34

$68,800 at 10¾% Fixed Rate interest & principal makes payment $642.59

$68,800 at 10¾% Graduated Mortgage Payment 6th–30th year $730.77

The reason for the higher payments on the GPM years six through thirty is because the unpaid interest was added to the mortgage balance making the mortgage balance larger after payments than when it first began. In other words, this is a negative amortization loan (See Definition on Negative Am. Loan)

INVESTOR

An investor loan is designed for a non-owner occupied home. As the word implies, it is the investor who owns the home and it is to him an investment. The requirements and guidelines are different on this loan than on an owner occupied loan. Generally, the investor loan requires a larger down payment.

NEGATIVE AMORTIZATION

Amortization is the liquidation (pay-out) of a loan, generally by monthly installment payments. Negative amortization of a situation in the loan agreement where the payments are not sufficient enough to pay off all the interest on the loan for the first few years. The unpaid interest amount is added back to the original loan amount. So, each year the loan amount increases rather than decreases until the monthly payment have increased enough to cover all interest and some principal. Negative amortization is usually associated with graduated payments.

QUALIFYING/ NON-QUALIFYING

Don't confuse these terms with "being qualified" for a new loan. The definitions, here, are in reference to more stipulations concerning an assumable loan. When assuming a loan with "qualifications" the buyer must meet requirements of the lender, as set forth in the loan agreement. The non-qualifying buyer does not need to meet any specifications. Another stipulation here is a "with or without release of liability" clause; the seller may still be held liable even with a qualified buyer, as set out in the loan agreement. This factor needs to be considered. The release of liability comes only from the investor through the mortgage company except with F.H.A., V.A. guaranteed mortgage loans.

Due On Sale Clause sets out guidelines or requirements whereby if not met the loan becomes due and payable in one lump sum; e.g., at the sale of the house the loan must be paid off. This clause is sometimes found in a qualifying loan agreement.

An F.H.A., V.A. qualified buyer releases the original buyer from liability on a loan assumption. The house can be sold non-qualifying, loan assumption, but it is best to know the buyer's credit history because the original buyer is still responsible to F.H.A., V.A. for the loan should the second buyer (the assumer) default. Effective December 1, 1986, all loans closed will have a provision which affects the assumability of these loans. Loans closed prior to that date are not affected by the change in the law.

RENT WITH OPTION TO BUY

This is a very good way to obtain a home, especially if a down payment is difficult. It is an agreement between a buyer (renter) and a seller (owner). As set forth in the agreement, the buyer has an option to purchase the house at a given time either by first right of refusal or other means. The first right of refusal gives the buyer the first option to buy the house before the seller puts it on the market. This sale can be at predetermined prices and financing or at current market value and financing that is available.

The most frequently used method of rent with option is when a set amount of the renter's monthly payment goes toward the down payment. This money that is put forth toward the down payment is usually forfeited should the renter not exercise his option to buy.

Even though the renter has been paying the seller, if the agreement calls for a new loan, the buyer must qualify with the mortgage company just like any other purchaser or he will, in most cases, forfeit any "option" (down payment) money. An assumable loan may also have qualifications.

Any option money can be taken off the sales price but not necessarily applied toward the down payment. If using this method for down payment money, on a new loan, the option agreement must meet the criteria of the lender or mortgage company in order for the money to be applied towards the down payment.

This is an excellent option when a buyer needs to buy and a seller needs to sell and the market conditions are not suitable, e.g., high interest. Waiting for the market to improve will provide the seller with better price and the buyer with better interest rate.

The number of different ways the rent with option can be structured is only limited by what the buyer and seller wish to accomplish and the recorded mortgage agreement that is in place at the time.

SECOND MORTGAGE

A self-explanatory term, it is simply the second loan on the same house. Most people think of a second mortgage as a way to get money for home improvement or college education.

In this book the second mortgage loan is referring to a way to buy a home that has an assumable mortgage. This loan is sometimes helpful when assuming a loan on a house with a low, non-escalating, interest rate. Usually, second mortgages are not gotten from a regular mortgage company. Sources can be found in the yellow pages under mortgages.

A second mortgage company will generally lend against the amount you have to put down. For example, if you have $10,000 they may lend you an additional $10,000. This would allow you to look for an assumable loan with $20,000 down rather than $10,000 down. The second mortgage opens up the market because the older the loan the more likely it is that it has a lower interest rate. A better assumable loan is one that has been paid on for several years.

Second mortgages have a higher interest rate than current first mortgage rates because the security of the second mortgage is not as good as the first. Should the second mortgage loan foreclose, the second mortgage company would have to assume obligations of the first mortgage. If the first mortgage loan forecloses, the second mortgage holder would either pay off the first mortgage or take over the payments to protect the investment. A second mortgage loan requires a three day waiting period before disbursement of funds under *regulation "Z" of the Truth and Lending Law.* This regulation will be discussed in chapter nine.

SHARED EQUITY

There are two basic types of shared equity: the first is a shared equity "loan" and the second is a recorded "agreement" between parties on an existing loan.

The shared equity "loan" is usually where the first party contributes all or part of the money necessary to obtain the loan and makes a contribution each month on the monthly payments. In exchange he receives a percentage of ownership in the house and a percentage of interest paid and property taxes that he may write off his taxes. The agreement between the parties would determine the amount of contribution and percentage of ownership.

A shared equity "agreement" is on an existing loan and depends upon the mortgage loan agreement and its stipulations. It would be a situation similar to this: a seller (investor) has a house, valued at $60,000, that he does not live in. He offers a buyer the opportunity to own half the house for a given down payment, say $1,000. Upon acceptance of the agreement the parties also agree that the buyer will:

1) make 100% of the monthly payments
2) do all upkeep and maintenance
3) pay for all repairs that don't exceed 1% of the value of the house
4) have 50% ownership

5) deduct 50% of the house, interest, and taxes from his own taxes

The investor:

1) must claim one-half of the monthly payment as income
2) deducts 50% of the house, interest, and taxes from his own taxes
3) deducts 50% of the fire policy off his own taxes
4) perhaps claim 50% of the repairs depending upon amount
5) can claim 50% depreciation

This is the way most shared equity agreements work. The agreement usually has a predetermined price for a buy-out by either party at any time. The standard agreement runs for about five years and can have a clause for a five year extension. Time limits are decided by the parties.

SWEAT EQUITY

By doing needed repairs or work on a home, a buyer can obtain some of the money needed to purchase the home. The home can be a resale or new construction.

The purchaser furnishes the labor (i.e. "sweat") and, perhaps, the material, depending on the agreement between the purchaser and seller.

Some lenders require that the work, on an existing house, be listed on the appraisal. If the lender is to count this "sweat equity" toward the down payment it must be 1) on the appraisal 2) by a purchaser who is qualified to do the work 3) at a reasonable cost 4) with an itemized cost breakdown submitted with the contract.

On new construction the work is not required to be listed on the appraisal but all other steps are usually required.

It is important for the buyer to have his loan approved before doing any of the work. Should the purchaser not be approved there might be some difficulty, unless seller agrees to pay the purchaser for his work regardless of loan approval.

V.A./VETERANS ADMINISTRATION

As stated in Chapter 2, V.A. does not make loans but rather guarantees loans to qualified veterans. The Administration backs the loans of family dwellings such as: single family detached, regular as well as mobile, single family attached (e.g., condominiums), fee-simple town-houses, duplexes, triplexes (3-family building) and quadraplexes (4-family building).

V.A. mortgages may be repaid in monthly payments over a term of 10, 15, 20, 25, or 30 years. Fixed-Rate, Graduated Payment and Growing Equity Mortgage (GEM) loan plans are available through V.A.

Does the VA make any loan directly to eligible veterans?
    Yes, but only to supplement a grant to get a specially adapted home for certain eligible veterans who have a permanent and total service-connected disability(ies). See VA Pamphlet 26-29-1 for information concerning specially adapted housing grants.

ELIGIBLE LOAN PURPOSES

You may use VA-guaranteed financing:

1) To buy a home
2) To buy a townhouse or condominium unit in a project that has been approved by the VA.
3) To build a home
4) To repair, alter, or improve a home
5) To simultaneously purchase and improve a home
6) To improve a home through installment of a solar heating and/or cooling system or other weatherization improvement
7) To refinance an existing home loan
8) To refinance an existing VA loan
9) To buy a manufactured (mobile) home and/or lot
10) To buy and improve a lot on which to place a manufactured home which you already own and occupy
11) To refinance a manufactured home loan in order to acquire a lot (See V.A. pamphlet 26-71-1 for more information about VA manufactured home loans.)

Can a veteran get a VA farm loan?

No, except for a farm on which there is a farm residence which will be personally occupied by the veteran as a home. The veteran may or may not conduct farming operations. If farming operations are to be the primary source of the borrower's income, then it must be established that the venture has a reasonable likelihood for success. If the borrower plans to use the residence, but has a source of income other than the farm which will be the primary source of income, then the farming operations need not be considered. Other types of farm financing may be obtained through the Farmers Home Administration which gives preference to veteran applicants. Additional information can be obtained by contacting a local office of that agency, the address and telephone number may be found in your telephone directory. VA Pamphlet 26-4, Dept. of Veterans Benefits

If the veteran is financing a mobile home with a permanent foundation, presently, V.A. will back the loan for thirty years. A manufactured home loan does require a 5% down payment as of February 1, 1988.

The Gramm–Rudman Law may cause many things to change, temporarily or permanently, so check with the V.A. or mortgage company to be informed.

OVERVIEW WITH EXAMPLES

Now for an overview. A buyer could have a mortgage loan agreement that was listed as an adjustable rate (payments usually change annually, based on market interest) and it could still have all the following associated with it:

☐ convertible (a provision to lock in the interest rate at a future date)
☐ an escalating clause (upon resale, payments may increase)
☐ a qualifying clause (new buyer would have to meet the mortgage company requirements)
☐ a conventional loan (not government guaranteed, e.g., FHA, VA)

☐ down payment was obtained by the "sweat equity" method (buyer exchanges his labor for some or all of the down payment)
☐ a conforming loan (the "loan" meets mortgage company specifications)

Confused? Let's try another example.

A buyer could have a F.H.A. loan (government guaranteed loan) and it would have the following associated with it in the loan documents:

☐ conforming loan (F.H.A. would not make a non-forming loan)
☐ non-escalating clause (upon resale, payments would not increase)
☐ no prepayment penalty clause (no fee to pay the loan off early)
☐ and is assumable (a new buyer can take over payments)

Less confused? Let's go, one more time.

A buyer could have a thirty year fixed rate mortgage (interest rate stays the same for 30 yrs) and could have all the following associated with it

☐ with a 3-2-1 buy down (seller buys down the first three years' payments, after such time they remain the same)
☐ conforming loan (the "loan" meets the mortgage company specifications)
☐ non-escalating (upon resale, payments do not increase)
☐ with prepayment penalty (loan paid off earlier carries fee)
☐ and assumable (a new buyer can take over payments)

Starting to get the picture? These are examples with different terms put together, merely for instruction purposes. They in no way are meant to imply that the things always go together, but they could, conceivably.

The structure or complexity of a loan document or agreement is important. A buyer today could be a seller tomorrow. The way a loan is structured has present and future importance. It is also important to understand the structure to know what has and might occur with monthly payments. For example, a buy down at first sight might look like a graduated payment but further observation will show that a true graduated mortgage usually has negative amortization associated with it. There are many other clauses in a recorded loan agreement which set out other terms.

LOANS TO AVOID AND WHY

Keep in mind that a house should be viewed like a savings account for the future and that interest and property taxes can be deducted from a person's income for tax purposes. Interest and property taxes are deductible to a degree but not dollar for dollar. If a person is in the 28% tax bracket (28 cents out of each $1.00 is paid in taxes) for example, and his interest and property taxes are $5,000 he would be able to deduct the $5,000 from his reported income and save $1,400 in taxes (28% of $5,000 = $1,400). Another benefit may be that the deductions will drop him into a lower tax bracket. An accountant can clarify this.

As much as there is to gain, there is also risk involved with homeownership. No one ever intends to have a house foreclose, but it is wise to strive for as many favorable terms as possible in your mortgage loan agreement. Foreclosure will affect the entire family. A smaller and/or cheaper house as a starter home may be the wisest thing to buy. All the benefits come with any house, e.g., tax deduction, investment.

If a loan has graduated payments, know what the highest payment will be. Consider your income now. Tomorrow is not guaranteed. Can you make the payments, with some ease, today? Are you relatively sure that the payments in five years will not cause hardships? Remember that, generally, the highest payment amount is the one you may end up paying for the longest amount of time.

The problem with a negative amortization loan may come when you want to sell. The amount of unpaid interest, which has been added back to the principal, may make the total that you owe more than the house is worth. It may be nearly impossible to find a buyer to assume the mortgage if you are in this situation.

SUMMARY

In this chapter we have tried to give you a better than average understanding of mortgage loans. We advise you to reread those things that seem confusing and of course read the rest of the book for even better understanding. All mortgage loans have advantages as well as disadvantages but the most important thing to keep in mind is that what's right for one person may not be right for another. Mortgage loans are very individual and require an educated buyer to decide what's right for himself/herself.

4

What About Caps, Indexing and Margins?

When talking about mortgage money, short term money is almost always cheaper than long term. Short term money is money that is borrowed from year to year. Cheaper means that the interest rate is less. Long term money is money that is borrowed for a longer period of time for repayment over a period, generally more than five years.

SHORT TERM MONEY

Short term money is actually safer for the lender because there is less time before the money is to be returned and, therefore, less time for the money market to make any major change. In this chapter "lender" is the more appropriate term but the home buyer generally never sees the "lender," only the mortgage company representative or "Mortgage Rep," who is the go-between.

But who can take out a $60,000 mortgage loan and pay it back in a year? This is where the adjustable rate mortgages (ARM) become so beneficial. The home buyer with an adjustable rate mortgage is basically playing the market year to year. With an ARM the loan is a trade-off; a lower interest initially, but assuming more risk that it can also go higher. The ARM loan is adjusted annually, sometimes semi-annually, for the life of the loan. For this reason a good ARM loan has "caps."

CAPS

Caps are limits placed on the interest rate. The first cap limits the amount of increase or decrease in the interest rate at the adjustment period. The second cap places a maximum and minimum interest rate that can be charged during the life of the loan. The maximum and minimums are referred to as *ceiling* and *floor*. Caps are given in percentages. A one percent cap with a lifetime of 5% means that the most the interest could increase or decrease at any one time is 1% and the interest could never increase or decrease more than 5% of the beginning interest rate. There are no set rules on caps. Different lenders offer different ARM programs.

The beginning interest rate is usually lower or cheaper on an ARM loan with no caps, but the home buyer will have no guarantee of the high or low of the interest rate.

INDEXING

How does a lender figure the change in the interest rate each year? The lender ties the interest rate to an "interest indicator," such as the one year United States Treasury Bill, or "T-Bill." This tie is called *indexing*. The lender can "tie" or index the interest rate to other sources. The index on a loan can be figured many ways. One way is on *weighted averages*. This is the total of up and down moves in interest rate for the previous year. By averaging these interest rate moves, the lender arrives at the weighted average. This information is then used to set the index. However, some lenders, rather than using the weighted average, may use the highest interest rate of the index that year or 90 days or so before the adjustment period.

MARGINS

The index is just the starting point to determine the interest rate. Then a percentage above this rate is added to come to the homebuyer's final interest rate. The *margin* is the percentage above the "indexed interest rate." The margin percent is added to the index to compute the next year's payments.

INDEXED INTEREST + MARGIN = HOMEBUYER'S INTEREST RATE
(This is referred to as "full indexed interest rate" in mortgage terms.)

So the buyer should carefully consider the indexing and margins of his loan. To repeat, it makes no difference what the loan is tied to if payments are the only consideration. This buyer is gambling and may lose it all, in other words, foreclose.

HIGH OR LOW OF THIS LOAN

Having gone through the previous definitions, determining the high or low of a loan is actually easier than you might think. For example, if a lender says he has a thirty year ARM with 9½% starting interest with a 1% annual cap and lifetime cap of 5%, what does he mean? Well, this means simply that the first year the interest is figured at 9½% interest. From year to year the most that the interest can go up or down at one time is 1% and over the life of the loan it can only increase or decrease a total of 5%. This makes a lifetime interest rate at a high of 14½% and a low of 4½%. The interest rate can move only one percent at a time regardless of the index. Caps in this sense are very protective and should be viewed like insurance.

Consider an ARM loan that has a buy down from the seller. In this case the interest rate is artificially lowered. The artificial beginning rate is not the rate that will be used to compute the remainder of the loan.

It is possible for the interest to change more than the caps because of the "buy down beginning." Conceivably, using a 3-2-1-buy down, with a 1% yearly interest cap and a 5% lifetime interest cap, interest could jump 6 percentage points in four years and still climb 2 more percentage points because the starting point was artificially lowered. It would seem as though the interest rate had risen more than the lifetime "cap" when actually it had not. The home buyer received a reprieve from the true interest rate.

This situation of a buy down on an ARM loan has caused many problems. Today, some lenders will not make such a loan. The payments have actually caused "sticker shock" and, in many other incidents, foreclosures. The spread presents too drastic a change in the monthly payments. The average home buyers will find it hard to adjust. It is advisable to be prepared. Perhaps the chart below will help to make the interest rate roller coaster more understandable.

The buy down is from a 9½% rate. As the index rate moves up, the 1% cap is applied to the 9½% starting rate. So payments go up each year for 3 years because of buy down. But payments can also go up 1% each year on the interest cap. So payments could conceivably go up 2% each of the first 3 years and still have 2% left to increase before reaching the lifetime cap.

In this example the interest index moves up each year for 5 years.

STARTING INTEREST RATE 9½%

ADJUSTMENT CAP 1%   LIFETIME CAP 5%

	Buy Down	Payment Rate With Buy Down	Starting Rate	Index Rate	Payment Rate
1st Yr.	3%	6½%	9½%	10½%	6½%
2nd Yr.	2%	7½%		11%	8½%
3rd Yr.	1%	8½%		11½%	10½%
4th Yr.	0	9½%		12½%	12½%
5th yr.	0			13½%	13½%
6th yr.	0			14½%	14½%

LOAN TIED TO WHAT?

Remember that "tied to" is indexing. It is important to understand what is happening. A buyer needs stability in the indexing of his loan. An index tied to a yo-yo index could certainly cause problems. Ask what the loan is tied to and also ask what the highs and lows have been for the last several years. This gives the buyer a better idea of what to expect in the future.

The margin actually sets the home buyers interest rate. As vital as the index seems the margin has the final word. Margin says that the interest rate will be x percent above the index.

CALCULATED INTEREST

Taking an example of a thirty year loan for $60,000 with monthly payments including principal and interest, the chart below shows what payments would be at a given interest rate.

6½%	$379.25	9½%	$504.52	12½%	640.80
7½%	419.53	10½%	549.00	13½%	687.60
8½%	461.35	11½%	594.60	14½%	735.00

Consider what a spread of five points can do to a monthly payment. A five point spread is a difference of over two hundred dollars in this example. When the loan has a 3-2-1-buy down attached the spread is even greater. To repeat what was mentioned earlier, when deciding upon a payment plan, take into consideration the highest payment as a guide not the lowest. Being able to make the lowest payments is not a wise indicator of your ability to make the highest payments. Today, most lenders will not use the ability to make the first year's payments to qualify a home buyer but instead they use the second year's payments. However, on a 2-1 buy down mortgage, companies will normally qualify buyers on the first year's payments. It is almost a sure bet that the second year payments will be an increase from the first even if interest stays the same. In fact this is true with most ARM loans, and will be covered later.

The starting interest rate on an ARM loan is usually one percent less than the current market index and margin at the time of the closing. There are basically two reasons for this: 1) the borrower might opt for a fixed rate loan if the incentive of a lower beginning interest rate was not given, 2) the lender does not want a temporary move down in interest to cause trouble with the yield on a loan with caps the following year. The next year's payment is computed on what the index interest rate does the current year and any quick moves up are hard for the lender to recover because of caps. Under regulation Z of the truth in lending law, mortgage companies are required to furnish a report of the past ten years on changes in interest rates, and the effect those would have had on the adjustable rate mortgage had it been made ten years prior. This is done to show the effects that such changes had on the adjustable rate mortgages and possible future changes.

LOAN CHANGES WHEN?

When dealing with F.H.A. on an ARM loan, F.H.A. sets the guidelines. The guidelines are the same for all lenders who do business with F.H.A. The percentages for margins and caps are predetermined as well as what the loan will be "indexed to" (tied to).

Taking a quick review, we know what caps mean and why they are important. Also we know why it is important to view what the loan is to be tied to or indexed to. Margin percents are important because they directly affect the interest rate of the loan. All ARMs do not start at the same interest rate.

If the main reason for getting an ARM loan is to get lower payments to qualify then the buyer is looking at the wrong loan and needs to consider lowering his expectations, i.e., a less expensive house.

An ARM loan can have a no-negative amortization or a negative amortization. A negative amortization loan has a payment cap but not an interest cap. So if the lender says there is a payment cap of 7½% a year it means that the payments, not interest, can increase by 7½% each year.

"Some mortgages contain a cap on negative amortization. The cap typically limits the total amount you can owe to 125% of the original loan amount. When that point is reached, monthly payments may be set to fully repay the loan over the remaining term, and your payment cap may not apply. You may limit negative amortization by voluntarily increasing your monthly payment. Be sure to discuss negative amortization with the lender to understand how it will apply to your loan."
(Federal Reserve Board)

5

What Is P.M.I.?

P.M.I. stands for private mortgage insurance. It is the private business equivalent to the F.H.A./V.A. home loan guarantee program. Some mortgage bankers and real estate agents refer to all mortgage insurance as *M.I.P. Mortgage Insurance Premium.* The P.M.I. companies guarantee loans that are *conventional,* that is non-government loans.

P.M.I. IS NOT LIFE INSURANCE

Don't confuse this mortgage guarantee with life insurance that pays off the mortgage should the owner die. These are two entirely different matters. The P.M.I. insurance is a guarantee, to the lender, that upon default, foreclosure, they will pay the claim. Claims are based on the percent of coverage that the lender has on the loan. This claim is paid to the lender. P.M.I. mainly protects the lender but indirectly benefits the buyer.

The private mortgage insurance companies insure a percentage of the loan to reduce the risk to the lender. The P.M.I. company pays this percentage to the lender if the loan forecloses. There are two ways that this payment may be done. One is to pay the lender the entire percentage as a claim to the lender. The other is to pay the lender all unpaid interest foreclosure costs, any other costs involved plus total amounts owing, in which case the P.M.I. company owns the house. Usually the company pays the claim and the house returns to the lender. Mortgage companies have the responsibility to use caution in the processing of a homebuyer's loan. If fraud is suspected, perhaps documents are changed or altered, the P.M.I. company may not pay a claim. Remember, the mortgage company is the go-between for the buyer but, at the same time, the buyer has a responsibility to the lender and the P.M.I. company that all representation is true and correct.

[45]

MORE THAN ONE COMPANY

There are many P.M.I. companies that insure mortgage loans for conventional lenders. It appears at first glance that the lender is covered from all angles. It is true that lenders rarely lose, but they must be cautious and informed lenders, if they are to continue to be able to lend money. Private mortgage insurance benefits the home buyer as well as the lender. When the lender's loans are insured he does not need to ask for a large down payment. If there were no mortgage insurance the lender would require larger down payments to reduce his risk. So you can see where the P.M.I. policies serve a two-fold purpose. The primary purpose is reduce down payments by insuring the lender's investment which in turn reduces his risk.

IS THIS ALWAYS NEEDED?

Lenders decide if they want private mortgage insurance. If they do want it, then it becomes a requirement of the loan. Some lenders do not require P.M.I. on a loan with a down payment of 20% or more of the selling price or appraised value whichever is less. Some lenders even require P.M.I. with a substantial down payment. These are some reasons that requirements differ on loans from one mortgage company to another. What a mortgage company can offer in home loans is limited to what their lenders and P.M.I. companies will allow.

If a loan is backed by F.H.A. or V.A., they set the requirements. If the mortgage company is using money from Fannie Mae or Freddy Mac the requirements would be set by these agencies. However, a mortgage company may require that a loan going to Fannie Mae or Freddie Mac have additional and/or higher requirements than required, because the loan does not meet the P.M.I. company requirements.

Why would a P.M.I. company want different or harder requirements? The P.M.I. company may feel that the risk on a particular type loan is too great and therefore increase the requirements.

GUIDELINES TO USE

The guidelines and standards of the P.M.I. company include the following: the amount of income against the monthly mortgage loan payment, income to total monthly obligations ratio, credit worthiness (underwriting guidelines or standards).

Lenders, the original source, mortgage companies, the direct source, and the private mortgage insurers, all have requirements. The home buyer must meet everyone's requirements and/or the highest standards that apply. Each type of loan will have its own set of requirements. The P.M.I. cost will be different on different types of loans. The cost of their insurance is based upon the risk. If records show that a particular type loan has had a high incidence of foreclosure then that type loan will carry a higher insurance premium, just like the cost to insure a teenage driver is at a premium, especially if he is driving a brand new Corvette.

In addition the P.M.I. company has different percentage amounts of the loan that they will insure. The higher the limit of coverage, the higher the cost. The lender sets the amount of coverage on the loan. It is a percentage of the loan amount that is insured in case of foreclosure. P.M.I. coverage, as an example, can go from 12% to 30% of the amount of the loan. Most loans on the market today with P.M.I. insurance are insured for 20 to 25% of the loan amount. In case of foreclosure the lender can collect his claim and resell the house. Many factors influence the cost of P.M.I., percent of coverage on a loan, the type financing and the amount of down payment.

When more than one person is buying a house, say in the case of a co-mortgager (co-signer), guidelines and requirements may be reduced for one, but both, together will have to meet requirements and guidelines. P.M.I. companies' guidelines and requirements change with market conditions and as the amount of risk demands. Market conditions include the interest yield and what the investor will gain. The interest yield changes almost daily. P.M.I. policies don't change daily but they do change when the market has been steadily influenced in one direction or another. The risk of a particular loan is determined by the number of foreclosures that have taken place in a given period of time with that type of loan.

REQUIREMENTS

Remember, V.A. insures a loan at no cost to the veteran. F.H.A. has a charge to guarantee the loan. This charge is collected in cash or it may be financed in with the mortgage loan. The cost for the mortgage insurance premium, if financed, is not considered as part of the loan and is added as an additional amount to the loan total.

P.M.I. companies charge a fee to insure a mortgage loan. The fee is usually a percentage paid in cash at the closing with the remaining percentage paid monthly along with the mortgage payment. Generally, there are no restrictions on who can pay, purchaser or seller, the cash premium at closing. There may be restrictions, however, on the amount that the seller can contribute to the total loan. All P.M.I. companies do not have the same rates, guidelines or requirements. The same factors that influence the percent of mortgage insurance also influence the cost of that coverage.

Private mortgage insurance insures a percentage of the loan balance. As the loan balance diminishes the percent remains the same. When the loan has a small balance owed, the P.M.I. still insures the same percentage. The P.M.I. coverage does not automatically come off of the loan when the loan balance reaches an 80% of value ratio. The loan may be paid down to 80% of the sale price but it does not release the P.M.I. company because the terms of the insurance for the lender were that a percentage of the loan be covered. Now that the remaining loan balance is down, the insurance covers that amount. In short the actual dollar amount changes in direct proportion to the dimishing loan balance but the percentage remains constant. Example:

25% Of $80,000 year 1 = $20,000 insured mortgage amount
25% Of $20,000 year 25 = $5,000 insured mortgage amount

The terms of the coverage are determined by the lender who states the requirements and whether the P.M.I. is to remain on the loan for the life of the loan. Regardless of other circumstances, such as down payment, the percent of P.M.I. coverage placed on the loan will always insure that percent of the loan.

The lender is the only one that can release the P.M.I. insurance on the loan. The mortgage company cannot do this without the approval of the lender. The P.M.I. companies are obligated by contract to keep the policy in effect for as long as is stipulated. There is a possibility that an agreement can be reached between the mortgage company, lender and buyer that at a particular point and time the P.M.I. can be cancelled. This would probably be when the loan balance was paid down to a certain amount.

The P.M.I. company may have a requirement on "gift" money for a down payment. Some companies require that if the borrower is receiving the down payment as a gift, perhaps from a family member, the borrower must also put down a payment of 5%. This shows, to the P.M.I. company, the stability of the borrower and reinforces, to the insurance company, his ability to pay.

The P.M.I. companies view "Rent with Option" and "Sweat Equity" situations very carefully when considering the down payment. Their main concern is whether the terms stated have actually been carried out. Some examples would be questions of this nature:
1) Is this the original rent agreement?
2) Has a sweat equity exchange actually taken place? (Or is someone trying to give the buyer the down payment?) A buyer who could not come up with the down payment is not a very good credit risk for the P.M.I. company. He is more likely to default on the loan. Remember, the lender and the P.M.I. company don't want to make any loans that would come back on them or foreclose. They want borrowers who will be faithful mortgage payers. Anything stated in the contract is considered to be enforceable by law and any misrepresentation could be considered fraud.

When shopping for a mortgage loan a person needs to ask not only about interest rates but also about other costs associated with the loan. Ask, too, about the P.M.I. coverage that the lender requires and the up front costs, at the closing, for the insurance and monthly premiums. Find out the length of time that the P.M.I. is required on the loan and if there is a clause to release it at a certain time.

Most P.M.I. companies offer two ways to pay for the up-front cash costs on the premium at closing. If the buyer wants to pay a lower premium in the beginning, he may be able to do so and have the monthly premium increased. Here again, remember that different lenders have different requirements concerning P.M.I. The total costs of P.M.I. coverage may vary from mortgage company to mortgage company. Most mortgage companies can deal with any P.M.I. company. P.M.I. companies have different requirements but the lender and/or investor has the final say in all respects. Mortgage companies deal with many different lenders and the lenders are not necessarily the same from one company to another. This fact can be an advantage to the home buyer looking for a tailored mortgage to suit particular needs.

6

What Are Points?

Points are a one time charge on the mortgage loan and they reflect stipulations on the interest rate. Points are also called *discounts or discount points.* Discount refers to the fact that points are a deduction from the main loan amount. They are the lender's and mortgage company's way of stabilizing an ever changing interest rate market. In the bond and money market, quotes on interest change several times daily. It would be a near impossibility for a mortgage loan company to quote this many changes to the home buyer. The changes are therefore adjusted by the discount points. The points are paid at closing to bring the yield on the loan to market rate.

INTEREST + DISCOUNT POINTS = YIELD

A lender does not usually lend out one dollar for one dollar. A dollar is lent out for fractions under the whole dollar amount. An example would be the dollar selling at 97.5 cents per $1.00. The difference is the discount which in this case is 2.5 cents, which is a 2½% discount.

1% = ?

Points are referred to in terms of "percent of" a loan amount. Discount points are based on the loan amount not the sales price of the house. Each percent or fraction thereafter is figured against the loan amount. For example if the market is at 2½ points, then, on a $60,000 mortgage the one time discount point charge would be $1,500.

Example: $60,000 × 2½% = $1,500

This amount is paid at the loan closing. It can be paid by the home buyer or seller except where state law would limit or prohibit and when dealing with V.A. The Veterans Administration states that the seller must pay discount points. When a veteran is refinancing his house he is both the buyer and seller and therefore pays the points.

[51]

IS IT ALWAYS TRUE?

One point is always equal to one percent of the loan amount. Sometimes a loan will not have discount points. One example would be when the market conditions are such that they are not required. Remember discount points bring the loan yield up to market rate and in some cases the yield is already satisfactory and discount points are not required. A market option frequently used is an increase in the interest rate, usually by fractions of percent, to offset the points needed to bring the loan to market yield. This is done quite often by mortgage companies. Mortgage companies might make a quote like "11% Interest Rate at 4 Discount Points, 11¼% at 2 Points or 11½% at No Points." These quotes are basically the same yield to the investor. This situation operates in reverse to a buy down. The fewer the discount points the higher the interest rate and conversely, by paying more points, the buyer brings down the interest rate.

FIGURED HOW?

The buyer and the seller have very little to say about the points that will be on the loan. These conditions in one form or another are dictated by the lender. Points are figured on yield. One percent in discount points is not equal to the yield that one percent of interest would bring over a thirty year mortgage.

$60,000 at 10% interest for 30 years will yield	**$189,648.00**
$60,000 at 9% interest for 30 years will yield	**$173,880.00**
Difference in interest for 30 years of yield	**$15,768.00**
Compare this to one discount point of $60,000 =	**$600.00**

Remember one discount point is equal to one percent of the loan amount.

A person can see very easily how impossible it would be to adjust any move in interest up or down if based on lifetime interest difference. Points help to make yield. Some mortgage companies base this yield on the number of years the loan may be on the books. So depending on the lenders and how many years they expect the loan to be on the books determines the number of discount points charged for 1% of interest. The average mortgage company calculates 5 to 8 discount points to be equal to 1% in the interest rate. The average mortgage loan stays on the lenders' books for about seven to twelve years.

YEARS TO BE ON BOOKS = NUMBER OF POINTS FOR 1% INTEREST

Basically, the higher the interest rate then the fewer discount points needed to equal one percent in the interest rate. The converse being true, the lower the interest rate the more discount points needed to equal one percent in the interest rate.

Let's look at 8 points as equaling 1% in interest. Therefore, 8 points would buy down the interest rate from 10% to 9%. On a $60,000 loan 8 points are equal to $4,800 ($60,000 × 8 = $4,800).

Let's see what the difference in interest would be between 8 and 12 years. On a mortgage loan of $60,000 the interest difference in a 10% loan as compared to a 9%, is $4,204 for 8 years and $6,307 for 12 years.

Look what happens if the lender put that $4,800 in the bank at 10% and let the interest compound. The lender would have:

$4,800 for 8 years@10% = $10,289 minus $4,800 = $5,489 Interest paid
$4,800 for 12 years@10% = $15,064 minus $4,800 = $10,264 Interest paid
$4,800 for 30 years@10% = $83,756 minus $4,800 = $78,956 Interest paid

If you are thinking about buying down the interest rate you may be better off putting the money in the bank.

BUT WHY?

Investors (lenders) will put their money where they can get the highest yield or return with the least risk. They prefer to be liquid, that is, to be able to sell at any time they need cash. Keep in mind that corporations through the sale of bonds, government through the sale of T-Bills, and others are competing for the same money in the market place. When a person enters the market looking for a mortgage loan he is now competing for the same money. The best security an investor can get is a government promise to pay. An investor can always sell the T-Bill in the market place. Anyone can pick up a newspaper and see the T-Bill rate. So, to compete for this money, the interest rate (yield) to the investor must be better than what a T-Bill is paying in yield, to entice the investor to put his money into mortgage loan yield. The interest rate is always moving in the market. The home buyer will see the moves reflected and adjusted accordingly, both in points and interest rates.

7

What Are Closing Costs?

When the purchase of a house goes from the construction loan of the builder to the permanent mortgage payments of the home buyer, there are costs involved to make this final. The *closing* is the paper signing at the attorney's office that makes the purchase legal. It "closes" the builder's construction loan and pays the bank any balance due, releasing him of any further monetary obligation. Also, in the case of a resale, the first owner, seller, is then released. Following, the buyer takes the responsibility to repay the money. He has now borrowed on the house, from the lender.

There are many costs involved in "closing" a mortgage loan. Many of these costs are in writing in the contract to purchase the house, and the amounts are stated on the sales contract. The costs written in the contracts are usually broken down into four parts: closing costs, discounts, real estate commission and pre-paid items.

APPRAISAL FEE

An appraisal is a necessary document to show the lender a reasonable estimate of value for loan purposes. A charge is made for the appraisal. F.H.A. and V.A. set the maximum charges for loans that go through their agencies. Conventional appraisers can set their own charges.

ATTORNEY FEE

This is a charge for all the paperwork that is required by the mortgage company. The attorney represents the mortgage company/lender and not the borrower or seller. Researching the title to the property is done for the lender's protection.

CREDIT REPORT

When a home buyer applies for a loan the mortgage company runs a credit check on the buyer. This is, of course, to verify credit worthiness.

The charge for this will vary, depending upon whether a local report is available to gather relevant information or if the report must be gotten from out of state. Credit reports in a loan package are normally good for 90 days. If the loan is in progress longer, then an update report is usually ordered.

ORIGINATION FEE

The mortgage company charges a fee for obtaining the borrower, home buyer, a loan. This fee is called an origination fee. Under F.H.A. and V.A. the fee is currently set, by the administrations, not to exceed 1% of the loan amount. On a conventional loan there is no set amount that the mortgage company can charge. The charge can be whatever the market will bear. H.U.D. (Housing and Urban Development) is considering allowing F.H.A./V.A. to increase this fee to as high as 3%. V.A. intends to maintain its charge at 1%. Currently, 1% of the origination fee can be financed in with the loan; this will stay the same.

POINTS = DISCOUNTS

Points were discussed thoroughly in a previous chapter. They are a charge by the lender through the mortgage company to bring his yield up to market rate on the mortgage loan.

SALES COMMISSION

This is the charge from the real estate company or builder's representative who sold the property to the home buyer. For the real estate company the charge is generally a percentage of the sale's price. The builder's representative may receive a straight fee per house. The seller usually pays this fee.

SURVEY

All land being sold must have a current deed. In the case of a home buyer the land will change hands from the seller to the buyer. This information is recorded at the county courthouse. An engineer must do the survey. A *plat* or survey is made to show the lot measurements and house with all easements and/or encroachments thereon for title purposes. This is done to be sure that the house and the lot being sold are one and the same. It also states that the measurements called for in the deed are the same and shows recorded or unrecorded easements or restrictions against the lot.

TITLE INSURANCE

The lender will require a title insurance policy. There is a one time charge for this. It protects the lender against any loss due to defects in the title of the property. Any claim that would cause problems with the lender's first lien on the property that was not detectable through the *title search* would be protected with the title insurance. This policy offers limited protection to the home buyer. A policy can be purchased to protect the new homeowner and it is called an *Owner Title Policy. There is a one time charge for this.*

OTHERS

These are some other costs that might appear on the closing statement. There may be others depending upon the mortgage company's requirements.

Assumption Fee: a fee for processing documents when one person assumes the mortgage loan of another.

Assessments: charges for unpaid improvements from the county or city, e.g. sidewalks, sewer lines or an annual fee for the homeowners' association, etc.

Inspection Fee: a charge for an inspection on work that was required on the appraisal or work on a new house that was not completed at the time of appraisal. Exterior pictures are required on all houses. There may be a charge for these pictures.

Recording Charges: The cost to record mortgage loan papers and the deed at the county courthouse in which the house is located.

Stamps: This is a tax imposed by the municipality, county, or state, on the deed and mortgage loan agreement upon sale or when a new mortgage is obtained. State law may say who pays these taxes.

Termite Inspection: A charge for a *termite letter or termite bond* which states that there is no wood damage or infestation of any kind from any wood destroying insects.

8

Prepaid Items Defined

Prepaid items are normally associated with buyer/borrower. They are costs associated with the borrower's payment and establishing an *escrow account* through the mortgage company for payment of taxes, insurance, etc.

ESCROW ACCOUNT

This is an account established at the mortgage company for the deposit of monies for taxes, insurance and so forth, which are paid by the home buyer and included in the monthly payments but become due only once a year. The mortgage company makes these payments for the home buyer. This arrangement is also called a *Reserve Account* or *Impound Account*. This escrow account is usually mandatory for loans that finance 80% or more of the sales price of the house. F.H.A. and V.A. require escrow accounts.

FLOOD INSURANCE

Flood insurance is required on a home that is located in a hundred year *flood plain* designated by the federal government. A regular homeowner's policy does not cover the damage from rising water of a creek or river. There is a regular yearly premium charge for this due in advance at the closing. This payment will be required for the coming year and also a payment for two months to be placed in the escrow account for the next year's premium.

HAZARD INSURANCE

This is the homeowner's insurance policy. The mortgage company will require that your first year's premium be paid in full plus two months put into an escrow account toward the next year's premium. One-twelfth of the insurance premium would then be included in the monthly payment. Be careful when shopping for a homeowner's policy for coverage. It is advisable to have a good policy with a higher deductible, which keeps down the cost of the policy, rather than a cheap policy with a low deductible and very little coverage.

An *HO3 policy with Extended Theft and Replacement Cost,* which stands for Homeowner's Number 3, is one of the best policies available because it offers very good value and greater protection than other policies.

INTEREST

The mortgage company will usually require that the borrower pay the interest on the loan through the last day of the month, in the month that the loan closing takes place. Mortgage payments are not made in advance but rather in arrears. For example, if the loan closed on September 15, then the borrower would pay interest through September 30. The first monthly payment would be due November 1. The November 1 payment is paying the interest that accrued in October.

MORTGAGE INSURANCE

This is the P.M.I. or F.H.A. required mortgage insurance that was discussed previously, not to be confused with life insurance on the homeowner that would pay off his mortgage in case of his death. F.H.A. has a payment that will cover the life of the loan. The P.M.I. companies have many different insurance payment plans. The most used plan is a two part pay plan; first, a cash premium paid at closing; then, monthly premiums included in the mortgage payments. Mortgage companies usually require two months' premiums in advance to be put into an escrow account.

TAXES

These are the real estate taxes levied on the home by the city and/or county. They are normally collected by the mortgage company which includes them in the monthly payment. At the loan closing the taxes are usually pro-rated, meaning that the seller pays his share of the taxes up to the closing date and the buyer pays from that date forward. The number of months' worth of taxes to be put into the escrow account is determined by the due date on the tax bill. For example, if the loan closing occurred March 30 and the tax bill was due on October 1, the seller pays three months, January, February and March taxes, and the buyer has nine months of taxes that will be due by October 1. Since the buyer's first payment is not due until May 1, which would pay for April, there is a remainder of four months' taxes due on October 1. At the closing, these four months' payments plus two for reserve would be payable, at the prerogative of the mortgage company. As a general rule the mortgage company collects two months extra on anything that needs to be paid out. This insures payment of the tax bill, which has a due date from the city or county, on time without regard to the time that the buyer might make his mortgage payment. The mortgage company has the funds, previously collected, to pay the bill in a timely manner.

The *RESPA,* Real Estate Settlement Procedures Act, sets the maximum amount that a mortgage company can require a buyer to deposit into the escrow account at loan closing.

In some cities and counties a deduction on taxes is allowed anyone living in his house as of January 1. This deduction is called *Homestead Exemption*. The homeowner must file for this deduction by a certain date or lose the exemption for that year. The closing attorney will know if this applies.

Property taxes are set from year to year. The assessment of the property and the tax millage rate of the city or county affect the total tax bill. Budget proposals are always changing so keep some extra money aside for our government.

OTHERS

Sometimes a loan is approved, provided the borrower pays off some other monthly obligation(s). The proof of this transaction will be required at the loan closing.

On occasion the seller has possession of the house until a certain date, after the closing. This might be especially true in the case of a resale. When this occurs the seller pays the new owner a portion of the payment to cover that time that he is still in the house. This amount is an agreement between the seller and buyer.

A copy of *Settlement Statement or Closing Statement* is found at the end of this chapter. It is the required settlement statement for F.H.A. and V.A. Most attorneys now use this form in lieu of all other forms for new mortgage loan closings. This form can be used as a guide once the home buyer has decided on a mortgage company and a home. It will assist in the calculation of money needed to purchase the house.

At the top of the form, spaces lettered "A" through "I" set out pertinent information on a loan and all parties involved in the loan.

Section J (100–303)	is a summary of the borrower's transaction.
Lines 101 to 105	set out sales price and costs to borrower
Line 102	is used if buying furniture, etc. (personal property; not real estate)
Lines 106 to 112	are used for paid in advance items which the buyer would owe a portion back to the seller, e.g., city / county taxes
Line 120	is a total of lines 101 through 112
Lines 201 to 209	are for monies that borrower has already paid, e.g., earnest money, and amount of new mortgage loan, or mortgage amounts that borrower is to assume
Line 210 to 219	amounts of which a seller would owe a portion back to the borrower, e.g., taxes
Line 220	the total of lines 201 to 219
Line 301	amount on line 120
Line 302	amount on line 220

Line 303	line 301 minus line 302
	This line shows the cash amount that the buyer needs to close out the transaction
Section K (400–603)	is a summary of the seller's transactions
Lines 401 to 412	set out sales price and money due to the seller
Line 420	total of lines 401 through 412
Lines 501 to 509	amounts that the seller owes
Lines 510 to 519	amounts which seller would owe a portion back to the borrower, pro-rated amounts, e.g., taxes
Line 520	total of lines 501 to 519
Line 601	the amount on line 420
Line 602	the amount on line 520
Line 603	line 601 minus line 602
	This shows the amount of cash that the seller will receive from the sale of the house

On the second page of the settlement statement is a summary that shows all costs involved in the mortgage loan and who is paying, seller or borrower (buyer).

Lines 700 to 705	states the real estate commission, due to whom and how much
Lines 801 to 811	states fees that may be due to the mortgage company
Lines 901 to 905	items required by lender to be paid in advance
Lines 1001 to 1008	items to be paid in advance to establish the escrow account
Lines 1101 to 1113	items that may be involved in title changes
Lines 1201 to 1205	costs involved with recording and transfer of all legal documents in connection with the mortgage loan.
Lines 1301 to 1307	list any additional requirements of the mortgage company
Lines 1400	the total of lines 700 through 1307
	settlement charges for seller and borrower/buyer

Settlement charges to the borrower are listed on line 103, Section J. Settlement charges for the seller are listed on line 502, Section K.

At the bottom of the second page both borrower/buyer and seller have a place to sign the agreement, to affirm that they accept the figures and amounts listed thereon.

There are a number of costs involved on a new mortgage loan. When shopping for a mortgage company, compare total charges along with the interest rate.

F. 2853-01 R 7/76   Form Approved OMB No. 63-R-1501   Page 1

A.		B. TYPE OF LOAN		
		1. ☐ FHA 2. ☐ FMHA 3. ☐ CONV. UNINS.		
		4. ☐ VA 5. ☐ CONV. INS.		
		6. File Number:	7. Loan Number:	
SETTLEMENT STATEMENT U.S. DEPARTMENT OF HOUSING AND URBAN DEVELOPMENT		8. Mortgage Insurance Case Number:		

C. NOTE: *This form is furnished to give you a statement of actual settlement costs. Amounts paid to and by the settlement agent are shown. Items marked "(p.o.c.)" were paid outside the closing; they are shown here for informational purposes and are not included in the totals.*

D. NAME OF BORROWER:
   ADDRESS:

E. NAME OF SELLER:
   ADDRESS:

F. NAME OF LENDER:
   ADDRESS:

G. PROPERTY LOCATION:

H. SETTLEMENT AGENT: I. SETTLEMENT DATE:
   ADDRESS:

PLACE OF SETTLEMENT:
   ADDRESS:

J. SUMMARY OF BORROWER'S TRANSACTION		K. SUMMARY OF SELLER'S TRANSACTION	
100. GROSS AMOUNT DUE FROM BORROWER:		**400. GROSS AMOUNT DUE TO SELLER:**	
101. Contract sales price		401. Contract sales price	
102. Personal property		402. Personal property	
103. Settlement charges to borrower (line 1400)		403.	
104.		404.	
105.		405.	
Adjustments for items paid by seller in advance		*Adjustments for items paid by seller in advance*	
106. City/town taxes to		406. City/town taxes to	
107. County taxes to		407. County taxes to	
108. Assessments to		408. Assessments to	
109.		409.	
110.		410.	
111.		411.	
112.		412.	
120. **GROSS AMOUNT DUE FROM BORROWER**		420. **GROSS AMOUNT DUE TO SELLER**	
200. AMOUNTS PAID BY OR IN BEHALF OF BORROWER:		**500. REDUCTIONS IN AMOUNT DUE TO SELLER:**	
201. Deposit or earnest money		501. Excess deposit (see instructions)	
202. Principal amount of new loan(s)		502. Settlement charges to seller (line 1400)	
203. Existing loan(s) taken subject to		503. Existing loan(s) taken subject to	
204.		504. Payoff of first mortgage loan	
205.			
206.		505. Payoff of second mortgage loan	
207.			
208.		506.	
209.		507.	
Adjustments for items unpaid by seller		508.	
210. City/town taxes to		509.	
211. County taxes to		*Adjustments for items unpaid by seller*	
212. Assessments to		510. City/town taxes to	
213.		511. County taxes to	
214.		512. Assessments to	
215.		513.	
216.		514.	
217.		515.	
218.		516.	
219.		517.	
220. **TOTAL PAID BY/FOR BORROWER**		518.	
		519.	
300. CASH AT SETTLEMENT FROM/TO BORROWER		520. **TOTAL REDUCTIONS AMOUNT DUE SELLER**	
301. Gross amount due from borrower (line 120)			
302. Less amounts paid by/for borrower (line 220) ( )		**600. CASH AT SETTLEMENT TO/FROM SELLER**	
		601. Gross amount due to seller (line 420)	
		602. Less reductions in amount due seller (line 520) ( )	
303. CASH (☐ FROM) (☐ TO) BORROWER		603. CASH (☐ TO) (☐ FROM) SELLER	

HUD 1 Rev. 15 76

L. SETTLEMENT CHARGES		PAID FROM BORROWER'S FUNDS AT SETTLEMENT	PAID FROM SELLER'S FUNDS AT SETTLEMENT
700. TOTAL SALES/BROKER'S COMMISSION based on price $ @ %=			
Division of Commission (line 700) as follows:			
701. $ to			
702. $ to			
703. Commission paid at Settlement (Money retained by broker applied to commission $ _____)			
704. Other sales agent charges			
705. Additional commission			
800. ITEMS PAYABLE IN CONNECTION WITH LOAN			
801. Loan Origination Fee %			
802. Loan Discount %			
803. Appraisal Fee to			
804. Credit Report to			
805. Lender's Inspection Fee			
806. Mortgage Insurance Application Fee to			
807. Assumption Fee			
808.			
809.			
810.			
811.			
900. ITEMS REQUIRED BY LENDER TO BE PAID IN ADVANCE			
901. Interest from to @ $ /day			
902. Mortgage Insurance Premium for months to			
903. Hazard Insurance Premium for years to			
904. years to			
905.			
1000. RESERVES DEPOSITED WITH LENDER			
1001. Hazard insurance month @ $ per month			
1002. Mortgage insurance month @ $ per month			
1003. City property taxes month @ $ per month			
1004. County property taxes month @ $ per month			
1005. Annual assessments month @ $ per month			
1006. month @ $ per month			
1007. month @ $ per month			
1008. month @ $ per month			
1100. TITLE CHARGES			
1101. Settlement or closing fee to			
1102. Abstract or title search to			
1103. Title examination to			
1104. Title insurance binder to			
1105. Document preparation to			
1106. Notary fees to			
1107. Attorney's fee to			
(includes above items numbers:			
1108. Title insurance to			
(includes above items numbers:			
1109. Lender's coverage $			
1110. Owner's coverage $			
1111.			
1112.			
1113.			
1200. GOVERNMENT RECORDING AND TRANSFER CHARGES			
1201. Recording fees: Deed $; Mortgage $; Release $			
1202. City/county tax/stamps: Deed $; Mortgage $			
1203. State tax/stamps: Deed $; Mortgage $			
1204.			
1205.			
1300. ADDITIONAL SETTLEMENT CHARGES			
1301. Survey to			
1302. Pest inspection to			
1303.			
1304.			
1305.			
1306.			
1307.			
1400. TOTAL SETTLEMENT CHARGES (enter on lines 103, Section J and 502, Section K)			

The above settlement statement is hereby approved, the disbursements indicated are authorized, and settlement may be completed by settlement agent.

Borrower _____   Seller _____

_____   _____

COMPANY

HUD-1 Rev. (5/76)

9

Behind the Scenes of a Mortgage Company

It is important to have some understanding of the inner-workings of a mortgage company before you shop for mortgage money so you know what questions you may need to ask and why.

MINIMUM REQUIREMENTS

Remember that the lender/investor will set minimum requirements on the funds used for mortgage loans. The mortgage company must use these requirements.

Fannie Mae, Freddie Mac and Ginnie Mae are sources of mortgage money and are, therefore, lenders. If the mortgage company is using these sources then the requirements from them apply to their loans. F.H.A. and V.A. insure loans but F.H.A. and V.A. also set the requirements on the loans that they are to insure. A mortgage company must comply if using these programs. P.M.I. companies have requirements that have to be met in order for them to insure a loan to the lender.

The mortgage company is a go-between and must meet requirements in all directions of loan sources. Federal and state laws have certain mortgage requirements too. One such provision in the *Truth and Lending Act of 1969* requires the lender to disclose to the borrower the annual percentage rate (APR), which sometimes tends to be confusing. The percentage rate is computed by adding certain charges that the borrower has to pay back to the interest rate. Under "Regulation Z" on refinancing and second mortgage loans there is a three day waiting period after the loan closing before the money can be disbursed. This is the borrower's *right of recision*. The borrower can change his mind and decide not to go through with the deal, but mortgage companies have no such right. Mortgage companies are obligated to comply with

[65]

the loan agreement. The intent of the act is to show all hidden charges and bring to light the true annual percentage rate. The borrower is given a three day period of grace. Unfortunately, there may be an occasion when the home buyer feels that things have been misrepresented to him. This waiting period gives the home buyer an alternative in such matters.

BUYING A COMMITMENT

A mortgage company stays in business by buying "forward commitments" on money to use for mortgage loans. These commitments are bought for a certain length of time. There are a number of sources for this money. Depending upon the wording of the commitment, the mortgage company follows the prerequisites of the lending source in respect to rising and falling interest rates. The mortgage company may be required to deliver loans to fill the commitment at the stated yield, even if the market rate is below that yield. Another option is a commitment that may adjust to the current market rate.

Commitment requirements may allow the mortgage company to forfeit money paid for the commitment in the event of non-performance on the part of the mortgage company. Forfeiting the money paid may be less of a loss than filling the commitment at the lesser yield. In other words, if the mortgage company was not able to fill the commitment at the stated yield and had no way out of the commitment, the company would have to make up the difference. There are also commitments that require a mortgage company to make monthly payments by a certain day, whether or not borrower / home buyer has made his payment by his required date. This is part of the risk / gain cycle of the business.

When a person looks at all the problems associated with a commitment it may be easier to understand why interest rates charged may move down a little slowly in reflecting a current rate quote. The most current quote is for the transactions taking place from that day forward. A commitment however, is made in the past, for future transactions. If a mortgage company had a commitment at a lower yield, they would probably make loans at the higher yield anyway, until the competition forced them to conform.

This is only one side of the story. What happens when interest rates start to go up? As previously stated, the commitment prerequisites will control, to an extent, what the mortgage company will be able to do. A yield may be at a given interest rate or another interest rate plus so many points. For example, 9½% interest rate and 4 points or 10% interest rate may be considered as having the same yield. Therefore the mortgage company could make loans at the stated yield of the commitment or they may be able to make the loans at a higher yield and keep the difference.

But in most cases the mortgage company reacts faster in a rising interest market when making loans. At the lower than market rate the mortgage company may not have a large enough commitment. In this case the mortgage company must make up the difference in yield to the lenders. It may be a prudent business decision. If market rates fall then the loan made at 11½% interest is worth a premium as compared to an 11% rate; but in a rising market, for example 12%, the 11½% is worth less.

Having completed a loan application does not necessarily assure a borrower of the going interest rate at that time. If interest goes down the buyer may get a break or if it goes up he may have to pay the price depending upon the real estate contract on the house. If a contract states *prevailing rate,* the rate that is most prevalent at the time of the closing, then the buyer has to pay the price (difference). If the application states a particular rate then it may be voidable at the buyer's option but this again depends upon the wording of the contract.

Depending upon the circumstances, it may take thirty (30) days to two or three months to get a loan approved and closed. Buying an existing house or having one built are also factors of time. No one can know in advance what the interest rate would be at that time.

Sometimes mortgage companies when taking the loan application will *lock in* the interest rate and points for a certain period. Some companies do this, but it is at the option of the mortgage company.

On occasion the mortgage company sells a commitment to a real estate firm or a builder. When this is done the company usually only locks in the points but not the interest rate.

ORIGINATING THE LOAN

Taking the loan application from the borrower, processing all papers and documents for the purpose of obtaining a loan and the closing of the loan are called *originating the loan.*

The mortgage company charges a fee for this "originating" but this fee generally covers only the cost involved. The origination fee is not a big money-making aspect of the mortgage loan business.

F.H.A. and V.A. set the maximum amount that can be charged for the origination fee. Conventional loan sources do not set a maximum that can be charged. If the mortgage loan money comes from a state or county bond, the maximum origination fee will probably be preset.

SERVICING THE LOAN

Usually the mortgage company that made the loan to the home buyer will collect or service the loan. As part of the servicing the mortgage company will:

- ☐ collect the monthly payments from the borrower
- ☐ make all necessary disbursements to the lender
- ☐ place all appropriate monies in the escrow account
- ☐ make all payments from the escrow account

The mortgage company receives a fee from the lender / investor for this work that has been predetermined by agreement. Again, F.H.A. and V.A. have minimum and maximum amounts that can be charged for this by the mortgage company that uses their services. This servicing fee is where the mortgage company receives another portion of its income. This is steady income from month to month. For this reason a mortgage company can break even on originating the loan and still make money on servicing.

WAREHOUSING?

A mortgage company does not receive money from the lender until the home loan has been closed. The mortgage company must put forward all the monies for the loan closing and then be reimbursed when the lender releases the money on / from the commitment.

This means that the mortgage company must have sufficient funds to carry on this intermediate transaction. A warehouse line, which is an amount borrowed from a bank, is the resource for the interim funds.

The mortgage company temporarily places completed loan documents as collateral into their line of credit at the bank. This is done while the documentation of a closed loan is prepared and readied to ship to the lender. As mentioned, the lender does not put up the money ahead of time and, sometimes, he may require that all of the commitment be shipped for reimbursement at the same time, rather than one loan at a time. Remember, commitments can be in increments of a million.

The mortgage company can make or lose money on the warehouse line. The warehouse interest rate, the interest that the company must pay the bank, is usually tied to the prime rate. When the mortgage company collects more in interest from the borrower than they are paying to the bank on the warehouse line, they make money every day that the money stays in the warehouse line. If the mortgage company is paying the bank more interest than they are collecting from the borrower, they are losing money.

In states where the law will permit, the mortgage company may use the escrow account as a compensating balance against the warehouse line of credit. This action will reduce the interest rate that the bank will charge the mortgage company on the warehouse line.

Some mortgage companies are owned by commercial banks or savings and loan institutions. They may be a source for mortgage money but they are usually no cheaper than any other source.

MEET THE MORTGAGE BANKER

The job of the mortgage banker is to make conforming mortgage loans. A conforming loan is one that meets underwriting standards of a lender / investor. A non-conforming loan does not meet these standards. The mortgage banker wants to make quality loans, in other words, loans that don't go into foreclosure. The mortgage banker certainly doesn't want a reputation with lenders or P.M.I. companies of having a high foreclosure rate. These companies are less likely to continue doing business with this mortgage banker.

A mortgage company can help or hurt a borrower. There is a fair amount of paperwork in processing a mortgage loan. Sometimes the mortgage representative inadvertently leaves out or misplaces an important document and therefore the borrower does not qualify. Observe the mortgage representative and his business organization. Remember that thirty years of good money will be placed in his care. Check his business against his own personal organization. Especially when a loan is marginal, meaning that it is a borderline case, right at or just under the requirements and guidelines, a mortgage representative may be able to go to bat for the home buyer and get the loan approved. Sometimes, one P.M.I. company may turn down the loan but another will take it. The conscientious mortgage representative will continue to try to get the loan for a marginal buyer who presented himself as creditworthy on paper.

At the same time, if the mortgage representative has a reputation of making bad loans, the lenders and P.M.I. companies may not want to listen to him plead the case of the marginal home buyer. A seasoned mortgage representative will know when to continue the struggle for the marginal conforming loan. A conscientious mortgage representative or real estate agent may be worth more to you than you may think.

Some mortgage companies have what is called a *direct endorsement.* This means that if the loan meets F.H.A. requirements and guidelines, then the company underwriter can approve the loan. An *underwriter* is a person within the mortgage company who has final say on the approval of a loan. For F.H.A. this approval is called *delegated.* V.A. calls this approval an *automatic.*

The more a mortgage company can do "in house," that is within their own company, the quicker the loan can be approved and closed. A mortgage company will not approve a loan that does not meet the requirements and guidelines. This would jeopardize their position. In the case of a marginal loan the mortgage company will send the loan package to F.H.A. or V.A. and let them approve or reject the loan.

Some mortgage companies have *in house appraisers or assigned appraisers,* exclusive to the mortgage company. This allows them to get an appraisal "in house" quickly, thus saving time on the entire loan package. V.A. does their own appraisals.

The mortgage banker grades the loans on a scale from excellent to very bad. This is done in two parts.
1) Property
2) Borrower—ability to repay loan and a grade from excellent to

poor on A) income to qualify
          B) credit history
          C) job stability and security

These criteria are what the mortgage banker will be considering. In a later chapter the topic of "How to View Your Own Loan" will be discussed in this way. The home buyer will know where he stands before he starts and what type loan would more likely be approved for him.

YOU SOLD MY LOAN?

A mortgage company commitment requirements may not allow them to service the loan. It may be that mortgage company does not have a commitment for your loan and is working through another mortgage company to place or fund the loan. The home buyer could go to the loan closing and be told to make his payment to a company he had never heard of because the loan had been sold to another company. The new company is now the servicing company.

Perhaps after the closing a notice comes in the mail telling you to make your payments to another company. This means that your loan has been sold. Remember that servicing on a loan is worth money. Servicing can be sold. The mortgage company may want to sell some loans to raise additional cash. Another reason could be that the loan came out of the warehouse line and was sent to the lender, who services his own loans.

When the home buyer thinks about a thirty year mortgage he does not realize that his mortgage may be bought and sold several times over its thirty year life. And so goes the money market, the buying and selling of "paper."

QUESTIONS TO ASK AND WHY

1) The first question is what type loan do I want? Then go after all the particulars of that loan. It would not hurt to ask if the mortgage company had anything better along the same line because there are many variations of the same type loan.

2) Ask what type requirements and guidelines apply to the loan and how will the mortgage company view them against my loan?

3) What are the particulars of this loan and do I understand them? With this knowledge you will know what to expect in coming years. Examples: escalating, qualifying and interest rate.

4) What about the mortgage insurance? Compare cost and amount of coverage.

5) What are the costs involved? Points, origination fee, etc. Compare the costs with other companies.

6) How long does it usually take the company to approve a loan?

7) How long until a closing?

8) Does the company have direct endorsements and assigned appraisers? This information may let you know that the mortgage company has a little more control over the total time it may take to approve the mortgage loan.

9) Will the mortgage company lock in the interest rate? Points? How long? This is especially important when building your home in a rising interest rate market.

10) Is the mortgage company also the servicing agent for the loans? Sometimes a non-servicing company charges more because the originating fee and discount points are their profit.

When asking about the costs involved on a loan remember that the market has a direct effect upon your homebuyer's cost. When the interest market is moving down the mortgage companies may need to make loans at a higher rate to fill a commitment. They may lower the rate but raise the points or charge an extra fee they don't usually charge. Again, if interest is moving up they might charge a warehouse fee to help offset the cost at the bank on their warehouse line of credit.

When asking for costs, the mortgage company may not be able to give the exact amount of the attorney's fees, etc. In most cases, you may not get a complete breakdown on closing costs but rather an amount that is a percentage rate of the loan amount.

In the final analysis, the costs you have to pay are the ones for your primary concern and not necessarily those that will be paid by the seller. Seller's costs are not as important for you to understand as the buyer's unless there is a stipulation that states that the buyer shall pay closing costs and/or points over a certain percentage.

Some mortgage bankers and loan officers are paid by salary, others with commission incentive or commission only. The way that the mortgage representative is paid can sometimes reflect on the points and costs that may be added. If the agent's pay is a percentage over the market rate, the buyer ultimately pays.

The real estate market is like a roller coaster and this means that the mortgage loan business is the same way. The current market conditions will have a bearing upon the quotes that you will receive. It will be hard to make a prudent decision unless you know the costs. If interest and points change and are not locked in, then you are almost back to square one.

10

How Much Down?

The amount of down payment depends upon the type loan and the size of that loan. For example, a house with a selling price of $80,000 with 5% down means a down payment of $4,000 leaving a mortgage loan of $76,000. The larger the sales price of a house the larger the down payment, generally speaking, because it is simply a percentage of a larger amount. And the reverse is true. The smaller the sales price the smaller the down payment. A 5% down payment on $50,000 is only $2,500. A loan with 5% or 10% down payment is also referred to as a 95% or 90%, respectively, loan to value ratio (L.T.V.). The down payment is not the only upfront cost to the buyer. If the buyer is paying the closing costs and the prepaid items then those are additional costs. It certainly would not be advisable to use all your savings to buy a home. That could place you in an unhealthy financial position.

This chapter attempts to establish the amount that you are able to pay for your home. This amount directly affects the down payment.

ANALYZE NEEDS

Although this book is on mortgage loans it is important to have an overview of all the costs involved in making your choice of a home. There is much more to the cost of homeownership than just being able to make the monthly mortgage payment. Other costs must also be considered.

The size of the family determines to some degree the size house that is needed. Sometimes the size of the family puts a limit on the amount that can be spent on the home because of existing expenses. Is the size of the family going to stay the same? That portion of income to be spent on another child will no longer be available for mortgage payments.

There are advantages as well as disadvantages to homeownership which depend largely upon a person's current situation. To most people a home symbolizes security, stability, achievement and it is an investment with tax advantages. On the other hand you have the responsibility of owning a house. You can't just pick up and go and must also be aware of maintaining the house and property. A house is like any other investment; it can turn sour, especially if the decision was not prudently thought out.

The very best place to begin to determine your needs is where you are right now. What are your current costs for housing? What do you like and dislike in your current housing situation? What about vicinity? What places would you like to be closer? Church? School? Different school? How about those matters relating to your safety like the fire department, emergency services, hospitals and police protection? Will you be changing jobs?

Remember, the further from work the more time in transit and the greater the transportation expenses. What is your family lifestyle? A yard for football? A small yard with a rose garden? Who will cut the grass? All these are things that need serious thought.

A larger home costs more now and in the future, this seems logical but then again, many people do not consider upkeep in the cost of home-ownership. There is a direct relationship between the costs of property taxes, utility costs, insurance, regular maintenance, replacement costs of things like roofing and the size of the house.

FORM: NEEDS VS. WANTS

This form is meant to be helpful in determining where to start. There can often be a gap between what you need and what you desire. One thing to consider in finding a home is the possibility and feasibility of additions. All houses are not suitable for additions. An added room cannot be placed just anywhere. Building codes may not allow this. If this is a consideration you will want to seek professional help. Don't just think you will add on a room at a later date; additions are not that simple.

Using the form that follows as *Step One,* try to be realistic and, at the same time, remember that anything can be justified that will improve your living: e.g., a dining room for the woman who loves to entertain, a large yard for a family with three sons, a study for the self-employed, a pool for the arthritic or a garage for someone with a '57 Chevy.

STRUCTURAL BASICS	NEED	WANT
Number of Bedrooms	_____	_____
Number of Baths	_____	_____
Size of Kitchen	_____	_____
Kitchen with Breakfast Area	_____	_____
Separate Dining Area	_____	_____
Living Room	_____	_____
Living Room/Dining Room Combination	_____	_____
Family Room	_____	_____
Playroom for Kids	_____	_____
Study	_____	_____
Sewing Room	_____	_____
Separate Washroom	_____	_____
Other	_____	_____
Other	_____	_____
Single Carport	_____	_____
Double Carport	_____	_____
Single Garage	_____	_____
Double Garage	_____	_____
Basement	_____	_____
Swimming Pool	_____	_____
Sundeck	_____	_____
Patio	_____	_____
Other	_____	_____

AMENITIES	NEED	WANT

(Some of these items may be supplied by an apartment complex and when buying a home you will need funds for these items; therefore they are included on this list)

	NEED	WANT
Built-in Vacuum	_____	_____
Burglar Alarm	_____	_____
Dishwasher	_____	_____
Dryer	_____	_____
Fire Detector	_____	_____
Freezer	_____	_____
Garbage Disposal	_____	_____
Garden Tub	_____	_____
Trash Compactor	_____	_____
Refrigerator	_____	_____
Sauna	_____	_____
Smoke Detector	_____	_____
Stove/Oven	_____	_____
Washer	_____	_____
Other	_____	_____
Other	_____	_____
SUB TOTALS:	_____	_____

Step Two of the form is to equate the above columns with a price index. To do this you need to find price equivalents to your *want house* and to your *need house*. This will give you an idea of what to expect your house or dream house to cost. You can get this information from the newspaper, real estate companies, builders and those free housing publications that are found at grocery and drug stores. Next, using the charts in Chapter 11, estimate the monthly mortgage payment for both "need" and "want" and enter amounts in "sub totals."

Step Three is a continuation of step one. To that step you need to consider the following yearly costs.

	NEED	WANT
Property taxes	_____	_____
Homeowners insurance	_____	_____
Electricity	_____	_____
Gas / Fuel Oil	_____	_____
Swimming Pool Maintenance / Heated Pool?	_____	_____
Water / Sewer Bills	_____	_____
Garbage Collection	_____	_____
General Maintenance / Repairs—Yearly Figure	_____	_____

SUBTOTALS: WANTS _____   NEEDS _____

(This amount should include materials and maybe labor on things such as yardwork, painting interior and exterior, cleaning carpets and carpet replacement, roofing. While roofing is only perhaps an every 20 year job, a prorated amount should be added here. The same for carpet and painting. These repairs can set a family's budget back and therefore need to be considered.)

Add the columns, one for needs and one for wants. Divide these totals by twelve to get the monthly needs and wants figures. Then add these last amounts to your previous subtotals. You can begin to see what your monthly budget will be for a new house. Also you should, by now, have a very good idea of the range of houses that will keep you within your budget. The stress of homeownership when not thoroughly thought out can be devastating, even unfortunately, to the point of foreclosure. This chapter was written to assist the homebuyer in avoiding this circumstance at all costs.

GRAND TOTALS: WANTS _____   NEEDS _____

Once you have decided on minimum needs, general location and maximum amount each month that can be budgeted towards the mortgage payment, you are well into your decision making. Now is the time to go househunting.

SHOPPING AROUND

There are two ways to begin looking for a house. First, ride the area taking down names and numbers off of "for sale" signs. Second, as mentioned before, look in the paper under "Homes For Sale," real estate companies, builders and homeowners who run ads. Sometimes the real estate companies and builders have special financing available. Remember, from an earlier chapter, this money may be available for a limited time because of the commitment from the lender. This may not be a "come-on" and should be taken seriously. Money that is available one week may very well not be available the next. You should know enough after having completed this book to tell for yourself if the money available is a come on or is for real. Just do your homework.

Keep in mind that the best price on a house is not always the determining factor of value. Consider the condition of the house, the age, its equipment and energy saving features. Don't be afraid to ask for work to be done or the price reduced if the work is needed, but be fair and honest. The last thing a new homeowner needs is a large repair bill. How long a person intends to stay in a house will help to determine the appropriate mortgage structure. If the homebuyer wants to resell in a couple of years he certainly wants an assumable mortgage loan.

11

Is Interest the Most Important Thing?

The question of whether interest is the most important part of your mortgage loan can be answered more easily now that you understand mortgage loan structure better. The answer certainly would depend upon the particulars that the buyer is looking for and his situation at the time.

There are situations where a higher interest rate might be the best deal. That is something that needs to be considered when the question of closing costs and discount points is mentioned. It is time to look at the total costs, not just the interest rate and who is paying, the buyer or the seller. When considering the best way to structure your mortgage loan all these items will be important.

In any given interest rate market, a fixed interest rate loan is the highest with maybe the exception of a graduated payment loan. The cheapest starting, but not necessarily in total costs, is the adjustable rate mortgage.

In this chapter you will see what different interest rates cost the home buyer/borrower. It will show how raising and lowering the interest rate through points can help. Even times of high interest rates can be used to the benefit of the knowledgeable home buyer.

AMORTIZATION: A FUNNY WORD

Amortization means to pay off a debt through installment payments. To understand this better let's look at the way a mortgage loan is paid off through monthly payments. This will show how much of the monthly payment goes toward the principal (loan balance) and interest. For this example the loan is $60,000 mortgage for thirty years at 12½% annual interest with monthly payments of $640.80, including principal and interest.

[79]

A 12½% interest rate is equivalent to 1.0417% a month, for all practical purposes, in mortgage banker terms. This rate per month can be determined by dividing 12 months into 12.5% annual interest rate. (12.5 ÷ 12 = 1.041666 rounded up to 1.0417% as a monthly rate)

		LOAN BALANCE
AMORTIZATION		$60,000.00
1st Month's Payment	640.80	
1st Month's Interest 60,000 × 1.0417% =	625.02	
1st Month's Principal Amount off Loan		
−(640.80 − 625.02 = 15.78)		
New Loan Balance after 1st Month's Payment		59,984.22
2nd Month's Payment	640.80	
2nd Interest Payment 59,984.22 × 1.0417% =	624.86	
2nd Month's Principal Amount off Loan		
−(640.80 − 642.86 = 15.94)		
New Loan Balance after 2nd Month's Payment		59,968.28
3rd Month's Payment	640.80	
3rd Interest Payment 59,968.28 × 1.0417% =	624.69	
3rd Month's Principal Amount off Loan		
−(640.80 − 624.69 = 16.11)		
New Loan Balance after 3rd Month's Payment		59,952.17

This process, when completed 360 times, will amortize (pay off) the loan.

CALCULATING INTEREST RATE: CHART

The interest chart below is for a $1,000 loan with monthly payments. It is calculated at various interest rates for either 15, 20, 25 or 30 years. For example: to figure an $80,500 loan at 12½% for thirty years, find 12½% on the left under annual percentage rate, go straight across on that line until you are under the 30 year column; this figure of $10.68 is the amount per month, per $1,000 for this loan. This example has 80.5 thousands, making the monthly payment $859.74 for thirty years. (80.5 × $10.68 = $859.74 including principal and interest)

Annual % Rate (APR)	15 yrs.	20 yrs.	25 yrs.	30 yrs.
7½%	9.28	8.06	7.39	7.00
8%	9.56	8.37	7.72	7.34
8½%	9.85	8.86	8.06	7.69
9%	10.15	9.00	8.40	8.05
9½%	10.45	9.33	8.74	8.41
10%	10.75	9.66	9.09	8.78
10½%	11.06	9.99	9.45	9.15
11%	11.37	10.33	9.81	9.53
11½%	11.69	10.67	10.17	9.91
12%	12.01	11.02	10.54	10.29
12½%	12.33	11.37	10.91	10.68

Annual % Rate (APR)	15 yrs.	20 yrs.	25 yrs.	30 yrs.
13%	12.66	11.72	11.28	11.07
13½%	12.99	12.08	11.66	11.46
14%	13.32	12.44	12.04	11.85
14½%	13.66	12.80	12.43	12.25
15%	14.00	13.17	12.81	12.65
15½%	14.34	13.54	13.20	13.05
16%	14.69	13.92	13.59	13.45
16½%	15.04	14.29	13.99	13.86
17%	15.40	14.67	14.38	14.26
17½%	15.75	15.05	14.78	14.67
18%	16.11	15.44	15.18	15.08

Using the figures from the above chart, take an $80,500 mortgage loan and calculate it for 15, 20, 25 and 30 years at 10%, 12% and 14% annual interest rate. Calculations listed below:

Rate per $1000

15 years at 10%	80.5 × $10.75 = $ 865.38	Monthly Payment
20 " " 10%	" $ 9.66 = $ 777.63	" "
25 " " 10%	" $ 9.09 = $ 731.75	" "
30 " " 10%	" $ 8.78 = $ 706.79	" "
15 years at 12%	80.5 × $12.01 = $ 966.80	Monthly Payment
20 " " 12%	" $11.02 = $ 887.11	" "
25 " " 12%	" $10.54 = $ 848.47	" "
30 " " 12%	" $10.29 = $ 828.35	" "
15 years at 14%	80.5 × $13.32 = $1072.26	Monthly Payment
20 " " 14%	" $12.44 = $1001.42	" "
25 " " 14%	" $12.04 = $ 969.22	" "
30 " " 14%	" $11.85 = $ 953.93	" "

It is easy to see that the higher the interest rate, the higher the monthly payment. But now let's look at the real difference in interest rates as reflected in the monthly payments:

Interest	15 yrs.	20 yrs.	25 yrs.	30 yrs.
10%	$865.38	$777.63	$731.75	$706.79
12%	966.80	887.11	848.47	828.35
14%	1072.26	1001.42	969.22	953.93

The next chart shows you the actual difference in 12% interest cost as the length of the mortgage loan is extended:

Years	Months	Payments	= Total Pmts	− less Mtg Loan	= Total Interest
15	180	$966.80	= $174,024.00 −	$80,500.00	= $ 93,524.00
20	240	887.11	= 212,906.40 −	80,500.00	= 132,406.40
25	300	848.47	= 254,541.00 −	80,500.00	= 174,041.00
30	360	828.35	= 298,206.00 −	80,500.00	= 217,706.00

In simple terms a loan for $80,500 for twenty-five (25) years at a payment of $848.47 a month would save $46,665.00 in interest over a loan for thirty (30) years. This savings only costs $20.12 per month more in the payments. So, from an interest standpoint it is cheaper by far to finance the mortgage for the least amount of time that your budget will allow. This would only apply, though, if you were planning to remain in the house for an extended time. Otherwise, increasing the payments to pay off the mortgage earlier may have no advantage.

USURY LAWS

Money is worth the amount that a person is willing to pay for it in interest. Some states have usury laws which state that interest shall not be charged above a certain percentage. A lender who does charge a higher percentage breaks the law. Loans acquired from federal government sources are exempt from state usury laws.

WHAT DOES A.P.R. MEAN?

A.P.R. is the abbreviation for annual percentage rate. The disclosure of the annual percentage rate became law with the Truth in Lending Act of 1969. It requires that the lender reveal the true interest rate with all charges added such as discount points, mortgage insurance and other charges collected by the lender.

For example, you may be looking at an 11% loan from a mortgage company but once all the charges are added to the 11% you find that the A.P.R. is actually higher. This is the part of the law that requires that the borrower be made aware of the "true" interest rate. Originally all charges, whether paid by the borrower or seller, were added together to figure the A.P.R. Now only those additional charges paid by the borrower are added in to figure the A.P.R.; if the seller is paying then they are not.

HIGH INTEREST RECESSION

High interest rates are usually associated with a slow down in the economy, sometimes called a recession. A knowledgeable home buyer can use this situation to his advantage. Hard times and high interest can be good times for the home buyer, believe it or not. First, look at some options a potential home buyer may have open to him in this type market. The seller who has an assumable mortgage may be willing to take some of his money as a second mortgage. If a house is vacant and has an assumable mortgage, the same circumstances may be available or perhaps a rent with option to buy which states all the terms of sale. This allows the buyer some time to wait for the interest market to improve.

If the buyer is short of cash the seller may be more willing, in a high interest market, to allow him to use "sweat equity" to obtain part of the downpayment or money needed to pay. Remember that high interest is based on supply and demand of money. High interest usually reflects a slow down in new homes being built. The number of home-buyers qualified to pay higher interest rate is limited. Therefore, when demand is down, meaning a shortage of buyers, prices usually come down. The seller who needs to sell is competing with other home sellers for a limited number of buyers. Generally, this drop in price will not make up the difference in monthly payments because you are dealing in a higher interest market. However, there can be other benefits.

Compare the $80,500 mortgage at 12% and 14% interest rate for 30 years.

12% monthly payments are $828.35
14%   "   "   " $953.93

The difference in interest charged is $125.58 a month.

The payment at 14% is $11.85 per one thousand dollars of the loan. At 12% interest the amount charged is $10.29 per month. In this example it would take a reduction in sales price of $10,597.46 to make up for the two percent in the interest rate to make the payments the same.

So how can a high interest market benefit the would-be home buyer? How can it be a good time to buy a house? In a good market, lower interest rates, houses are not usually reduced and the seller does not want to pay all the closing costs or the discount points because the ball is in his court. He has the buyers in a lower interest market.

Making the right decision involves a few questions in order to structure the right mortgage loan in this type market.
1) Does the seller have a loan on the house now? What type of loan?
   Number of years left on the loan? Loan balance? Interest rate?
   Is the loan assumable? Will seller let someone assume?
   Is it an escalating or non-escalating loan?
2) Is the interest rate climbing?
   Does it appear that interest has reached its peak?
   Has interest leveled off?
   Is interest headed down?

Now, take a seller who has a home that is appraised for $80,500. The seller is willing to sell for $75,900, pay up to 3% of the closing costs and pay discount points which are at 4%. The seller is also willing to have a buyer take over his remaining mortgage balance of $36,840 at 10½% for twenty years. The monthly payments are $407.18 plus taxes and insurance.

Example:

Appraisal	$80,500
Seller's Price	75,900
10% Downpayment	7,600
Loan Needed	68,300
Less 4% Discount points paid by seller	2,732
Less 3% Closing costs also " " "	2,049
The seller mortgage balance	36,840

Net amount to seller with downpayment of $7,600 is $34,279. This is the amount that the seller is really looking for and if a person can come up with this amount then there is a sale. The sources for some of this money may be a second mortgage company. Perhaps the seller will take back part of this as a second mortgage. This situation can be done in a good market. However, the seller may not need to be as cooperative.

Let's take another way to work this loan. Take the market rate at 14% annual interest with 4% discount points and interest continuing to climb. Remember, when interest is changing, discount points are not stable either.

Appraisal	$80,500
Seller's Price	75,900
Buyer's 10% Downpayment	7,600
Loan Needed	68,300
4% Discount Points	2,732
Closing Costs	2,049

Monthly payments for a 30 year loan of $68,300 at 14% interest is $809.36; this is principal and interest but not taxes, insurance, or mortgage insurance. Now seeing this, what about getting a mortgage company to raise the interest a little to take care of the discount points that would be due them. In other words, the amount of the discount points that would be paid by the seller would now be paid by the buyer in increased interest. At the same time the seller would reduce the price of the house by the amount that he would have paid in discount points. All the way around the yield is basically the same, just gotten in a different way. Depending upon the loan commitment, if the market is at 14% then the new rate would probably be about 14½% annual interest. You may have to try more than one company to get one to go along with this suggestion.

Seller's Asking Price	$75,900
Seller's Acceptable price $75,900 − 2732(Dis.Pts) = $73,168	
Buyer's 10% Down Payment	7,320
Loan Needed to Finance	$65,850

Monthly payments at an annual interest rate of 14½% are $806.66. This is for thirty years and includes principal and interest.

Your monthly payments in this case, not all cases, are less by raising the interest rate and doing away with the discount points. This particular payment is $2.70 less and the borrower/buyer owes $2,450 less on the mortgage. Down payment is reduced by $250. The interest is also a tax deduction. There are times when this action is very beneficial.

Please keep in mind that a loan will not always work out this well. This is an alternative to be considered and checked out. See if your loan could apply. Find out what the differences would be. All this is preliminary work and should be done before signing the contract with the seller. If the market is a "seller's market" the price may be raised on such a loan. However, if the market trend favors the buyer, then the opposite may apply. Another important consideration is the type of original loan on the house. Does it have a "Balance Due Upon Sale" clause? Will there be an assumption of the original loan? If this is the case, you will certainly want to obtain a thorough title search and survey, to be absolutely sure that there are no easements on the lot or house that may interfere with your plans, and that the title is free and clear of any other indebtedness or liens.

When the interest market is climbing, try to get a commitment on interest and points. Interest and points are subject to change before a loan can be approved and closed. When interest rates are going higher the discount points will go up first. Following this the interest is raised then the points begin to rise again before the interest rises again. This procedure is repeated until the market tops out. That is when the rates are so high that selling comes to a near halt.

The movement at either end of the interest market is usually not as fast or drastic as it is in the middle range. It is always a good idea to try to get a commitment on the interest rate and points unless you feel for certain that the market is going to improve. Even the experts do not do well when guessing the interest and points on quick, short moves from week to week. When interest is dropping, the points drop off first before there is another move down in the interest rate. Then, with the next interest drop, the discount points begin upwards and then make the trip back down before interest moves again. This is usually the cycle of interest rate changes.

It is easy to see that a potential home buyer really needs to be well informed. A little knowledge can be harmful, so continue to ask questions and seek answers. This mortgage market is no place to gamble. Make sure that you can meet the requirements for the present interest rate and discount points. Try to get a commitment on interest and discount to protect yourself. If the market improves the mortgage company may pass the benefits on to you but at the least you have attempted to lock things in so that they do not get worse.

The good points of a bad market (high interest) are that sellers usually drop prices and are more receptive to alternative methods of financing. This does not mean that the buyer should try to take advantage of the seller but it is a buyer's market. There must be some advantage to each party or there is no incentive to be creative. A house that has been purchased with a discount in price could possibly be refinanced to lower the interest rate at a later date.

PRIME RATE/ FLOATING RATE

Most construction loans are tied to the prime rate. This means that the rate being charged begins with the prime rate as a base and a charge is made above that. This is sometimes called a *floating rate* because the interest rate can change from month to month. This type loan cannot be assumed but must be paid off. It is a short term loan of six months to a year for building.

Builders sometimes have commitments on money and better rates, in a high market, because of this. When mortgage companies have commitment money that is about to run out, they will tell builders and real estate agents to push for a sale so that all may benefit from the better interest rates or points. This is a reminder to the home buyer that commitments do not last indefinitely and they may be gone in a week or two.

If the market rate is going up and a builder's sales are falling off, a buyer may be able to get a better deal. A good rule of thumb to measure a "good deal" is to compare appraised value against sales price and the items that the builder is willing to pay, e.g., closing costs, discount points.

12

Your Qualifications:
How to Figure the Loan Amount You Can Qualify For

Mortgage companies, P.M.I. companies, F.H.A. and V.A. have requirements and guidelines. They are not necessarily the same unless the same lenders and P.M.I. companies are involved. Through mortgage companies, F.H.A. will qualify a person using guidelines in a particular way. V.A. will qualify the veteran in a different way and conventional loan companies have their own set of requirements.

After these personal qualifications, each type of mortgage loan, like an ARM or graduated payment, may have another set of requirements that are exclusive to it. Guidelines and requirements can also change when market conditions dictate that they should.

FINDING THE BEST LOAN PACKAGE

The home buyer first needs to determine the type mortgage loan that best suits him. Then the buyer needs to find a mortgage company that has the best loan package for this type mortgage. The home buyer will need to know the requirements and guidelines of the mortgage company and those of the mortgage loan, in order to figure the amount that he can qualify for. Ask the loan company if they have any other loans that are similar to or better than the one you are asking about, in reference to the entire loan package. For example, sometimes the municipalities will sell bonds for mortgage loans. The interest rate is usually lower and this would be one reason for looking into this. The potential home buyer must know where he stands financially. What amount of income can be put towards the housing allowance? What are the present total monthly obligations? What debts will count against the amount they will be able to borrow?

The husband's and wife's incomes are counted, but sometimes the wife must have been on the job more than a year for her income to be counted. An exception would be if she had just finished college and gotten a job. Another consideration is whether or not the wife will continue to work in the event of childbearing.

A rule of thumb on gross income is that a person needs to make $4.00 for each dollar of the monthly mortgage payment and $3.00 of income for each dollar of total monthly obligation including the monthly mortgage. Taking an honest, objective look at your present finances cannot be over stressed.

By filling out the following form you will be on your way to knowing just what you can handle. First, put down what you actually spend now for housing. Then, complete the monthly salary section including all deductions. Gross income won't get it here. Fill in all fixed monthly debt payments and the number of months that are left to pay for them. This is the time to consider the value of these items should they be sold. The cash section is to be anything that can be liquidated or turned into cash without much trouble. This would include such things as a boat or car, if they are paid for. Otherwise, these things are liabilities and should be listed under obligations.

Now, go back to the form in chapter ten on needs and wants. You can use these amounts to complete the anticipated housing expenses section and also the extra cash needed section of this new form. When you fill out the "needed" items section of this form, consider those things that you must have upon immediate occupancy, e.g., a stove or refrigerator. Check with a local store to get a realistic price quote.

FINANCIAL FORM

Housing Expenses Now

Rent (or) mortgage payment	$_____
Electrical Costs	$_____
Heating Costs	$_____
Water and/or Sewer Cost	$_____
Renters/Hazard Insurance Policy	$_____
Any Other Costs	$_____
Monthly Total	$_____

Income

Monthly—Husband's Salary	$_____
" Wife's Salary	$_____
Any Other Income	$_____
Total Monthly Income	$_____

Deduction

Federal Income Tax	$_____
" " "	$_____
State Income Tax	$_____
" " "	$_____
Social Security or Other	$_____
" " "	$_____
Insurance (Health, Life)	$_____
" Other	$_____
Any Other Deductions	$_____
Total Monthly Deductions	$_____
Total Net Monthly Income	$_____

Monthly Debts:

Car Payments	$_____ # of months left ____	Value $_____
" "	$_____ " " " ____	" $_____
Installment Pmts.	$_____ " " " ____	" $_____
" "	$_____ " " " ____	" $_____
" "	$_____ " " " ____	" $_____
Other Debts	$_____ " " " ____	" $_____
Total Monthly Debts	$_____

Other Monthly Obligations:

Contributions/Tithing	$_____
Child Care	$_____
Car Expenses/Gas	$_____
Car/Parking	$_____
Other Transportation Costs	$_____
Life Insurance	$_____
Health Insurance	$_____
Car Insurance	$_____
Medical Care	$_____

FINANCIAL FORM (CONT.) _____

Monthly Food Costs	$_____
Meals Eaten Out	$_____
Clothing	$_____
Entertainment / Recreation	$_____
Other	$_____
Total	$_____

Total Net Monthly Income	$_____
Total Debts and Obligations	$_____
Any Remainder for Savings?	$_____

Cash Reserve:

Checking Account #1	$_____
Checking Account #2	$_____
Savings Account	$_____
Whole Life Insurance	$_____
Bonds	$_____
Stocks	$_____
Pension Fund	$_____
Other	$_____
Total Available Cash	$_____

Anticipated Housing Expense

Total Monthly Mortgage Payment	$_____
(Principal, Insurance & Taxes)	
Electrical Cost	$_____
Heating Costs	$_____
Maintenance	$_____
Water / Sewer Costs	$_____
Other	$_____
Monthly Total	$_____

Cash Needed:

Anticipated Down Payment	$_____
" Closing Costs	$_____
" Pre Paid Items	$_____
" Discount Points	$_____
Total Cash Needed to Purchase	$_____

Needed Items:

Refrigerator	$_____
Stove	$_____
Washer	$_____
Dryer	$_____
Furniture	$_____
Drapes	$_____
Lawn Mower	$_____
Other	$_____
Total Amount of Needed Items	$_____

For a moment let's just look over this form. Do the amounts listed under cash needed on the "anticipated down payment" line and the other lines for anticipated cash needs total more or less than the amount that is in the cash reserve section? Is the anticipated housing expense section more than the present housing expense section? If so, is there enough to cover the additional monthly cost in the section "other monthly obligations" on the line "any remainder for savings"?

Perhaps these figures have brought a startling truth to light. Maybe the figures show that you will need to adjust your "wants." There may be some debts that need to be paid off, more money saved, or some assets sold to bring things into line. Either way, you now have a realistic picture of your financial condition.

Now that you have your gross and net income figures and your total monthly debts you can see just what you can afford from the budget for housing expenses. If the cash is a little short you may want to try to find a home that already has some of the things on your want list: for example, a house where the seller leaves the stove and perhaps the drapes.

When you are looking in an area, find out what has been the common practice concerning closings costs and points. If you find that sellers have been paying these costs, this fact may save you money. F.H.A. will add closing costs and finance this in with the loan as long as it does not exceed the maximum loan limits.

The seller of a house cannot contribute more than 6% of the mortgage amount towards the sale of an F.H.A. loan (effective 1988). The buyer must pay all the charges above the 6% figure. This 6% figure would include discount points, buy downs, closing costs, and the mortgage company loan origination fee. There is an exception that applies if the contract states that the buyer and seller agree on an interest rate move up solely as a result of a change in market conditions. In this case, the 6% rule will not be imposed because the market change is considered an unplanned buydown. At present V.A. has no limitations on the seller's contributions.

If the market conditions are such that these costs are more than 6% of the mortgage loan, you may want to see if the mortgage company will reduce or eliminate the discount points by raising the interest rate. You also need to see if the seller will reduce the price proportionately; if it is the practice in the area for the seller to pay discount points, then this alternative should be considered, especially if the buyer is having to pay the discount points. However, this action may be part of the buydown requirements, depending on the type of loan involved. The 6% figure may, at times, be adjusted up or down, based on market conditions, so check it out first with the mortgage company.

**GUIDELINES:
"26/35" WHAT?**

A mortgage company may refer to their guidelines as *underwriting standards* or *underwriting guidelines*. "26/35" is one of many qualification ratios used on income to potential monthly housing cost and income to total monthly obligations. Simply put, the first number is a percentage multiplied by your monthly income and the resulting amount is your guideline to which you will be held. The same is done with the second number. Your guidelines are then measured against your potential mortgage loan figures. The housing cost will always include the mortgage payment and mortgage insurance. In addition this cost may include items such as taxes, hazard insurance and estimated maintenance and utilities. Whether or not the additional items are included in this figure depends upon the lender and mortgage insurer's guidelines.

"26/35" is used here only as an example. In qualifying ratios the first number will always be smaller than the last.

The first number measures the percent of income against the potential monthly housing cost. The second number is the percent of income against total monthly obligations which includes the previous amount of the potential housing cost.

An example of this would be a family monthly gross income of $3,100, which is multiplied by the first number, in this case 26%.

$$26\% \times \$3,100 = \$806.$$

The monthly housing cost cannot exceed this amount. Next,

$$\$3,100 \times 35\%, \text{ the second number, is } \$1,085,$$

the total monthly obligations including the mortgage housing cost cannot exceed this amount. So for this example 26/35 is also equal to $806/$1085.

Once the computations have been done the comparative figures must be gotten. The $806 above is the maximum amount that total housing cost can be. Conventional loans generally use the mortgage payment of principal and interest (P.&I.), property taxes on the house, homeowner's insurance policy and the P.M.I., premium, all added together to get the monthly housing cost. Then this is figured against the $806 or monthly income. Gross or net income may be used depending upon institutional guidelines. F.H.A. will add the above items plus estimated maintenance and utilities. F.H.A. will use the housing cost against net income rather than gross.

Total monthly obligations are debts. Conventional loan sources usually do not count a debt that will pay out in ten months or less. However, some mortgage companies count any debt over six months. Credit cards may have the minimum payment applied to debt obligations for the regular user. Many conventional loan companies do not use child care as a debt. An association fee, as in the case of a condominium or

PUD, which is a required contribution to the upkeep of a common facility or area, is counted as a monthly housing expense.

Usually F.H.A. does not count a debt that will be paid off in six months or less. Credit card debt is handled the same way unless it is excessive. Child care, for any children under age thirteen, is figured as a monthly obligation. For F.H.A. purposes these amounts are added together to get the total monthly obligation and then figured against the net income. F.H.A. ratios will be larger than conventional because net income is used in the computations rather than gross.

Generally V.A. counts any monthly obligation over six months toward the monthly debts. The V.A. total monthly obligation also includes maintenance, utilities, child care and mortgage payment against net income. V.A. will use other factors to determine a loan approval for the veteran. V.A. now also uses ratios, and all debts are used to calculate the balance of "funds available for family support."

However, F.H.A. has a new rule in the making for determining income qualifications for the mortgages they insure. The new method is expected to use "gross income" instead of "net effective income." The new ratios will be set at 29% and 42%, and items like heat and utility costs will no longer be considered in the expense column. The purpose of the new rule is to parallel conventional lenders and thereby increase the number of qualified buyers for Section 203(b) mortgage insurance.

It is important to understand just what the mortgage company will count as debt against you. You will need to ask the representative exactly what items are used for the calculations and whether they are figured against net or gross income. How does this particular company view child care and credit cards?

The buyer needs to know if there are any limits on the seller's contributions toward the sale. Just what do they define as a contribution? If a seller is paying closing costs and discount points on a loan, this action may be considered a contribution. The mortgage company may have limits on the amount that a seller can contribute. In some cases, the buyer must pay when the seller has reached the limit, even though the seller is willing to contribute more.

If contributions do exceed a predetermined limit it may be wise to raise the interest rate enough to do away with the discount points and lower the sales price by that same amount. In this way the contribution may meet the mortgage company's allowable limits. This was discussed in chapter eleven.

Qualifying ratios will vary some, from mortgage company to mortgage company and from one type mortgage loan to another. Within limits, there are always exceptions to any rule. For example, if the applicant has a considerable amount of cash in the bank, the mortgage company may look at the overall qualifying in a different light. If the first income ratio was a little high but the second income ratio was low, meaning that there was little or no debt, the loan would probably be approved anyway.

The following are excerpts from a Veteran's Administration's bulletin on guidelines concerning income and maintenance qualifications. They may serve as a good reference guide, but are strictly a guide and not a rule book. The most accurate information and updates on costs must be obtained from the mortgage company and V.A. The Veteran's Administration has implemented major changes since the first writing of this book.

> The current major provision is a two-tier guideline for underwriting their loan applications. The tier is intended to recognize that less income is needed to support a lower loan, specifically loans in the amount of $69,999 or less. In addition to providing a lower tier of residual income guidelines, all of the figures, including those for loans of $70,000 and above, have been updated based on the most recent data supplied in the "Consumer Expenditure Survey" published by the Department of Labor, Bureau of Labor Statistics.

> In making a credit determination for a V.A.-guaranteed loan, it should be borne in mind that a veteran's benefit is involved. The law intends that the veteran have this benefit provided that the requirements of the law are met. However, it serves no purpose to approve or make a loan to a veteran who will be unable to meet the repayment terms or is not a satisfactory credit risk. Current monthly rental or other housing expense is an important consideration when compared to that undertaken in connection with the contemplated housing purchase.

The circular from which these excerpts have been taken is twenty pages long and only a small portion of it has been presented in this book. Any veteran wishing to use the full benefits of his eligibility should seek personal advice directly from the nearest Veterans Administration office.

TABLE OF RESIDUAL INCOMES BY REGION *
(FOR LOAN AMOUNTS OF $69,999 AND BELOW)

†Family Size	Northeast	Midwest	South	West
1	$348	$340	$340	$379
2	583	570	570	635
3	702	687	687	765
4	791	773	773	861
5	821	803	803	894

*Table subject to periodic changes, consult V.A. for most current figures.
†For families with more than five members, add $70 for each additional member up to a family of seven.

TABLE OF RESIDUAL INCOMES BY REGION *
(FOR LOAN AMOUNTS OF $70,000 AND ABOVE)

† Family Size	Northeast	Midwest	South	West
1	$401	$393	$393	$437
2	673	658	658	733
3	810	792	792	882
4	913	893	893	995
5	946	925	925	1031

*Table subject to periodic changes, consult V.A. for most current figures.
†For families with more than five members, add $75 for each additional member up to a family of seven.

GEOGRAPHIC REGIONS

Northeast — Connecticut, Maine, Massachusetts, New Hampshire, New Hampshire, New Jersey, New York, Pennsylvania, Rhode Island, and Vermont

Midwest — Illinois, Indiana, Iowa, Kansas, Michigan, Minnesota, Missouri, Nebraska, North Dakota, Ohio, South Dakota, and Wisconsin.

South — Alabama, Arkansas, Delaware, Florida, Georgia, District of Columbia, Kentucky, Louisiana, Maryland, Mississippi, North Carolina, Oklahoma, Puerto Rico, South Carolina, Tennessee, Texas, Virginia, and West Virginia.

West — Alaska, Arizona, California, Colorado, Hawaii, Idaho, Montana, Nevada, New Mexico, Oregon, Utah, Washington, and Wyoming.

INCOME LIMITS AND FAMILY SUPPORT

MAINTENANCE AND UTILITIES

Maintenance and utility costs are based on the square footage of the home. Factors such as the age of the home, structure, air conditioning, energy efficient features and other relevant factors can be considered in determining the cost.

SQUARE FOOTAGE	Up to 1200	1201-1600	1601-2000	2001-2500	2501-3500
MAINTENANCE	35	40	45	50	75
UTILITIES	105	135	145	165	210
(TOTAL)	140	175	190	215	285

PUDS / CONDOS — Use the association fee + utilities + ½ of maintenance charge above.

MULTI-UNITS — Add 25.00 / month to above schedule for units not occupied by veteran.

SWIMMING POOLS — Add 75.00 / month.

CHILD CARE COSTS

When the veteran and spouse are both employed, have young children and the amount of child care expense is not stated on the application,

VA will automatically include the following charges for child care:

ONE CHILD	TWO CHILDREN	THREE OR MORE
$180	$330	$400

V.A. currently uses a two-part system for underwriting veteran's loans. One is a *modified residual income* method and the other is a *debt-to-income ratio* approach. At the first writing of this book the V.A. did not use ratios; however, with increasing foreclosures of V.A. loans, alternatives were sought to improve the system.

The *modified residual income* method uses the veteran's monthly income and deducts regular monthly expenses. The amount left over must fall within a particular range for qualifying. The location of the house and the number of people in the family are also considered in the qualification process.

When the *debt-to-income ratio* is used, insurance, homeowner's association fees (if any), principal, taxes, and interest, plus debts that extend beyond the next six months and major job related expenses like child care are all lumped together and must not exceed 41% of gross monthly income. The 41% figure fluctuates around certain parameters, but it is a strong baseline. Any approvals beyond the 41% require approval of officers further and further up the ladder as the percentage climbs above the 41% mark. Mortgage companies are also required to give appropriate reason for lending above the baseline. V.A. states that both systems are to be used congruently, and that no veteran should be denied a loan based on only one approach.

Consideration can be given for single veterans. A lower minimum requirement can be used.

These figures are furnished as a guideline only. Other important factors to be considered are:

a. The borrower's demonstrated ability to accumulate liquid assets (e.g., cash, bonds).
b. The borrower's demonstrated ability to use credit wisely and to refrain from incurring an excessive number of debts.
c. The relationship between the proposed shelter expense and the amount the borrower is accustomed to paying.
d. The number and ages of the borrower's dependents.
e. The locality and economic level of the neighborhood where the property is located.
f. The likelihood of increases or decreases in borrower's income.
g. The borrower's work experience and history.
h. The borrower's demonstrated willingness and ability to meet voluntarily incurred obligations in the agreed-upon manner (e.g., making payments on time).
i. The amount of any down payment made.

A veteran must have sufficient verified liquid assets to support the loan and to pay for his portion of any closing costs, prepaids (including costs paid outside of closing, such as an insurance policy) and a reserve of one month's payment to cover moving expenses, utility hook-up charges and unexpected expenses.

WOULD YOU MAKE A LOAN TO YOURSELF?

When examining your mortgage loan application you should consider the following subjects with all candor and honesty. Some of the subjects are the very same factors that the mortgage company and the P.M.I. company will be scrutinizing.

Credit History	Excellent — Good — Fair — Poor
Ability to Save	Excellent — Good — Fair — Poor

One of the best ways to survey your possibilities for a particular mortgage loan is to assume the role of the mortgage company. Would you lend mortgage money to yourself?

1) Is this loan in line with the ratios? You would want to know that there is enough income to support the family as well as pay the mortgage payment. This is the reason for qualification ratios.

2) Is the credit rating good? Do you feel that with this rating the possibility of foreclosure would be very unlikely?

3) Has the applicant demonstrated the ability to save? There is a certain discipline and sacrifice to saving. Or, are they over-obligated even though paying on time?

4) Is the family income sufficient to handle the difference in housing costs? Will this new obligation put the family at a financial disadvantage?

5) Is job stability represented? If there have been job change(s), have they been consistent with career growth?

6) Is there some semblance of job security?

7) What is the family situation? Newly married? First child? Last child? Anyone in college?

8) Are there adequate funds to close the loan? Will any money be left? Would a new debt be created, should there be a need for additional funds?

9) If there will be a significant increase in monthly housing payments, will it be handled sufficiently by the family income?

10) Are the ratios close?

There are some very specific questions that may need to be answered concerning the credit history. These questions would be the same concerns of the mortgage company.

A) Is the present credit rating good but the past rating shows some real problems?

B) Was there a very good reason for the poor credit rating in the past? For example, severe illness or accident, or lay-off from a formerly stable job like auto manufacturing or airlines company?

C) Does the overall report reflect an effort to be conscientious and creditworthy?

Now, after having taken yourself through the wringer, it is time to address the big question. Would you make a loan to yourself?

RIGHTS CONCERNING YOUR CREDIT REPORT

The Fair Credit Reporting Act states that the consumer is entitled to a "summary" of his own credit report but it does not grant the right of on sight examination or inspection. This summary will make reference to the structure and material in the report.

The report may have a section called the "investigative consumer report." Neighbors and friends give reference concerning their opinions of your character and actions.

The validity of your credit report can be challenged. And, in the case of error, it is your right to demand correction. For additional information on your credit report rights, contact the Federal Trade Commission (FTC) in Washington, D.C., or the nearest FTC office.

There is a due date on almost all bills and therefore a person knows if the bills have been paid on time. If the bills have been paid anytime after this date the report may state the actual number of payments paid after the due date and the exact day that it was paid. It may state "slow to pay" or "poor" when a creditor states that notices or calls have been made to collect the bills. Sometimes this sort of payment behavior will produce an "unsatisfactory" standing with this creditor. This is certainly a bad sign of creditworthiness and may be cause for rejection by the mortgage company. If you have been arrested, filed for bankruptcy, been sued, have outstanding judgments or any pending litigations, this also may be on your credit report.

Under the *Real Estate Settlement Procedures Act* (RESPA) the mortgage company representatives are no longer at liberty to discuss, with the potential home buyer, the credit report. The applicant must first go to the credit reporting agency and review the report and then the mortgage company involved can discuss the report with him.

Prior to the RESPA the mortgage representative could advise the clients on things to do to make their credit more acceptable. In the past a mortgage representative may have told you to pay down a certain bill so that it would not count against you. Now, the loan package is sent to the underwriters who will then advise the mortgage company on what if anything the client might do to improve their chances for approval. An example would be that your extra funds are sufficient to pay off one of your obligations and you may be approved subject to paying off that obligation. If the funds were not verified as being available to pay off this obligation you might be turned down. The government has given something and at the same time something has been taken away.

FIGURING MONTHLY PAYMENTS

The total monthly payment is determined by the mortgage loan amount, interest rate, number of years financed, mortgage insurance premium, property taxes, hazard insurance premium, flood insurance premium (if required), and association fees (where applicable). Maintenance and utilities are also going to be costs.

If a buy down is used on a loan how will it affect the monthly payment from year to year? A graduated payment plan mortgage will have yearly effects on the budget and this needs to be understood. In the case of an ARM, adjustable rate mortgage, what is it indexed to? Is there a cap? What is the total rate? Is is a negative amortization?

Loans could be named anything but the real question is what does the loan provide? Someone could say that he has a loan called "Ultimate 2" but what does it actually provide for the buyer? Is it just a fancy word or worse a coverup for low beginning payments with a high negative amortization? A potential home buyer needs to know the pertinent questions to ask to determine the actual type loan that is being offered. These questions are:

1) Is the starting interest rate and accruing interest rate the same? If one interest is charged and another rate is used to compute the interest you are looking at a negative amortization loan.
2) Does this loan have a cap on the interest or are the payments capped?

If the payments have limits and the interest does not then the loan can still be a negative amortization loan. Loans can be packaged to produce the desired results. Many times it is a matter of merchandising to make a product appear far better than it really is. Beware of any loan that appears to be too good to be true because, in all likelihood, it is not a loan that favors the home buyer.

Payment shock is a consideration of anyone involved with loan placement. F.H.A., P.M.I. companies and mortgage companies are judicious when the homebuyer's monthly housing expense will go up dramatically. They will seriously consider the buyer's ability to save and if this was not possible at a lower expense it is hard to see that it could be done at a higher one. It is possible for a buyer to qualify in all other areas and be turned down on this one item because the change is too drastic. The buyer has a right to talk to F.H.A. and V.A. about a loan rejection, but a mortgage company representative must accompany him because the company must show that they support the buyer.

On the following pages there are different ways to work the same mortgage loan. The examples will show how various programs may fit into a homebuyer's needs.

EXAMPLES OF VARIOUS PROGRAMS

For all examples these statistics remain the same:

House has 1250 Sq.Ft.
Appraised Value of House is $72,500.
House is Selling for $71,900.
Seller is Paying Closing Costs
Seller is Paying Discount Points of 4%
Property Taxes last year $ 760.
Hazard Insurance will be $ 445.
Buyer's Gross Income Is $ 3,000.
Buyer's Net Income Is $ 2,410.
Buyer has in Savings $ 7,100.
Two Children in Family
Child Care per Month $ 350.
Car Payment $ 147.   18 months left to pay out
Furniture Payment $ 42.   5 months left to pay out
Credit Card Minimum Payment $ 12.   Balance of $68.
Credit Card   "   " $ 15.   Balance of $260.
Credit Card —— $ 00.   Used in last 30 days
Credit Card —— $ 00.   Used in last 45 days

EXAMPLE #1

FIXED-RATE MORTGAGE

30 years at 10½%
Conventional loan
95% (L.T.V.)
Discount Points—4
1st Year P.M.I. = 1%
Monthly P.M.I. = 0.35%
Qualifying Ratios 28/36
Gross Income Used

Credit Cards—Minimum Payment
Credit Cards—$10 used in last 60 days, with -0- balance
No Maintenance
No Utilities
No Child Care
Monthly Housing Costs—use principal & interest. P.M.I., insurance and taxes
All debts over 6 months counted

On this example the down payment is 5% of the sales price ($71,900).

.05 × $71,900 = $3,595.00 rounded up = $3600

(Mortgage companies usually lend in increments of $50.)

Taking the down payment from the price leaves $68,300 for the loan.

$71,900 − $3600 = $68,300

To compute this monthly mortgage payment you multiply $68,300 by $9.15. This is from the chart on amounts per thousand dollars of loan amount.

$$\$68,300 \times \$9.15 = \$624.50$$

The property taxes were $760 for the year so divide this by 12 for a month and add this amount to the previous monthly total.

$$\$760 \div 12 = \$63.34$$

Continuing to compute your monthly payment you figure the hazard insurance using the yearly premium of $445

$$\$445 \div 12 = \$37.09 \text{ per month}$$

Next is the P.M.I. insurance computed at 0.35% of the loan value

$$0.0035 \times \$68,300 = \$23.91 \text{ per month}$$

The final monthly payment is $748.84. May be rounded to $749.00

The monthly payment is computed but there is much more to be done.

For the example the monthly income for the husband and wife is $3,000 gross. In order to determine if this couple will meet the first qualifying ratio of 28, this computation is done:

$$\$748.84 \div \$3,000 = 24.961333 = 24.96\%$$

The percent of 24.96 is less than 28% so the income qualifies the couple, on the first part of the ratio.

The second qualifying ratio is total monthly debt against monthly income. For example, this family has:

1) Car Payment — 18 months left to pay it off		$147.00
2) Furniture — 5 months left to pay off, not counted		(42.00)
3) Credit Cards — $260 balance, minimum payment		15.00
$68 " " "		12.00
No balance but used in 60 days counts		10.00
" " " " " " " "		10.00
4) Child Care — not counted by this mortgage company		0.00
5) Others — company not counting any other		0.00
Sub Total of Total Monthly Obligations		$194.00
Add Mortgage Payment		$748.84
Total Monthly Obligations		**$942.84**

The second ratio is determined by dividing the total monthly obligations by total monthly income:

$$\$942.84 \div \$3000 = 31.428 = 31.43\% \text{ ratio}$$

This figure of 31.43% is lower than the qualifying figure of 36%, so here again, the couple meets the requirements.

The seller is paying the closing costs and discount points but the buyer must have cash on hand for his part of the closing expenses. The mortgage company has asked for eight months of taxes to be placed in escrow. This couple has $7,100 in savings and checking.

$$8 \text{ (months)} \times \$63.34 = \$506.72$$

The interest adjustment for the amount due from the buyer is going to be a prorated share through the fifteenth of the month. This data is used just for example. It is computed this way:

$$\$68,300 \times 10.5\% = \$7,171.50 \text{ per year} \div$$

$$12 \text{ months} = \$597.63 \div 30 \text{ (days)} = \$19.92 \text{ per day}$$

$$15 \text{ days} \times \$19.92 = \$298.80 = \text{Buyer's portion of interest}$$

To figure the hazard insurance portion that would be required for cash needed, take the monthly premium of $37.09, as computed before,

$$2 \text{ (months)} \times \$37.09 = \$74.18 + \$445.00 \text{ (1 yr. prem.)} = \$519.18$$

The P.M.I. is 1% of the loan amount of $68,300, to compute:

$$0.01 \times \$68,300 = \$683.00 \text{ (1 yr. prem.)}$$

To figure the P.M.I. portion that would be required for cash needed, take the monthly premium of $23.91, as computed before,

$$2 \text{ (months)} \times \$23.91 = \$47.82 + \$683.00 \text{ (1 yr. prem.)} = \$730.82$$

The total cash needed by this couple to acquire this house is $5,655.52. This leaves $1,444.48 cash remaining which is an important factor to the mortgage company. It would not look good for the closing expenses to drain all available cash. Basically, with all other things in order, job stability and good credit, this couple has qualified to buy the house.

Any of these five factors could have caused a rejected loan application:
1) Ratio #1
2) Ratio #2
3) Job Stability
4) Credit History
5) Cash on Hand
Loan approval is a multifaceted process.

EXAMPLE #1-A   **Interest Raised to do away with discount points**

$68,300 Mortgage Loan × 4% Discount Points = $2,732

$71,900 Sale Price − $2,732 = $69,168

$69,168 New Sales Price × 5% Down Payment = $3458.40

$69,168 Sale Price − $3458.40 Down Payment = $65,709.60

$65,709.60 rounded down to the nearest $50 = $65,700.00

$65,700 Mortgage Loan, Down Payment $3,458.40 = $3,468.00

$65,700 × 11% ($9.53 per $1000) = $626.12 monthly payment

$65,700 @ 11% + No Points $626.12 = Down Payment $3,468

$68,300 @ 10½% + 4 Points Costs $624.50 = Down Payment $3,600

Benefits: Down Payment is $132 less

Payoff loan is $2600 less

Total cash for 30 yrs. is $1.62 per month = $583.20

If the mortgage company will reduce or eliminate discount points by raising the interest rate and the seller will reduce the price proportionately, then this alternative should be considered, especially, if the buyer is having to pay the discount points.

EXAMPLE #1: Completed Loan Form

Conventional Fixed Rate Mortgage Loans
95% – 90% – Other L.T.V. (loan to value)

Sales Price   **$ 71,900.00**   Qualification Ratios* **28/36**
(Minus) Down Payment **$ 3,600.00**   Interest Rate **10½%**   D. Points **4**
Mortgage Loan Amount **$ 68,300.00**   × rate per 1,000 **$ 9.15** = M/P&I* **$ 624.50**
Mortgage L/A **$ 68,300.00** × P.M.I. Premium due at closing **1.00%** = **$ 683.00**
Mortgage L/A **$ 68,300.00** × monthly premium **.35%** = **$ 23.91**

Monthly Payment:

*Principal and Interest	**$ 624.50**		
$\frac{1}{12}$ Property Tax	**$ 63.34**	Yearly Property Tax	**$ 760.00**
$\frac{1}{12}$ Hazard Insurance	**$ 37.09**	Yearly Hazard Insurance	**$ 445.00**
Monthly P.M.I. Premium	**$ 23.91**	Due at Closing P.M.I. Premium	**$ 683.00**
Other	**$ N/A**		
Total Monthly Payment·	**$ 748.84**		
+ Estimated Maintenance	**$ N/A**	is mortgage company counting this	
+ Estimated Utilities	**$ N/A**	is mortgage company counting this	
*Total Monthly Housing Costs	**$ 748.84** ÷	**$ 3,000.00** =	**24.96%**

Income net or **gross**   House to Income
*ratio (28)

Monthly Debt:

*Total Monthly Housing Costs	**$ 748.84**		
Debt Over (6 Months)	**$ 147.00**		
Credit Cards	**$ 47.00**		
Child Care	**$ N/A**	is mortgage company counting this	
Other	**$ N/A**		
Total Monthly Debt	**$ 942.84** ÷	**$ 3,000.00** =	**31.43%**

Income net or **gross**   Debt to Income ratio (36)

Cash Needed To Close:

Down Payment	**$ 3,600.00**	*Pre-Paid Items	
*Pre-Paid Items	**$ 2,055.52**	Hazard Insurance + 2 Months	= **$ 519.18**
If Paying Closing Costs	**$ Seller Paying**	Due at Closing P.M.I. + 2 Months	= **$ 730.82**
Other	**$ N/A**	Taxes #8 of Months?	= **$ 506.72**
Total Cash Needed	**$ 5,655.52**	Interest #15 of Days?	= **$ 298.80**
Do you have cash above this amount?		Total Estimated Pre-Paid Items	**$2,055.52**

EXAMPLE #2   **A.R.M., Adjustable Rate Mortgage**

  1) Starting at 8½% interest rate

  2) 30 years

  3) Indexed to the costs of funds for the Farmer's Home Loan Bank (This rate does not fluctuate as much as others)

  4) Yearly cap 1% — Lifetime cap 5% on interest

  5) Margin 2%

  6) Discount points 5%

  7) Qualifying Ratios 25 / 33 on 9½% interest rate

  8) 95% L.T.V.

  9) 1st Year P.M.I. = 1.25%

 10) Monthly P.M.I. = 0.40%

Most A.R.M. loans will have a slightly higher discount and P.M.I. premium. P.M.I. companies consider their risk greater; however, with a large down payment, the risk is lessened, and the P.M.I. rate comes down.

In this example everything is the same pertaining to the mortgage loan as it was in example number one except this example is an adjustable rate loan. All the particulars have been stated previously. The mortgage company index and margin total 9½%. The beginning rate of 8½% is not used to qualify but the 9½% rate is used. There is no negative amortization because interest is capped, not payments.

In order to better understand these examples, take time to go back over example number one, compare the figures and see where the changes have been made. The biggest difference in the two loans is the difference in payments. The payment for this loan at 8½% is $525.23 but if the interest increases to 13½% the payment goes to $782.72, a difference of $257.49 per month.

EXAMPLE #2: Completed Loan Form
Conventional
Adjustable Rate Mortgage Loans (A.R.M.)
95% – 90% – Other L.T.V. (loan to value)

Index Rate Now **7½%**	Qualification Ratios* **25/33**
Margin **2%**	Starting Interest Rate **8½%** D. Points **5**
Total **9½%**	Is This a Higher Rate than Starting Interest Rate
Yearly Interest Cap **1%**	Life Of Loan Interest Cap **5%** + **8½%** = **13½%**
	Starting Rate Highest Rate

Sales Price **$ 71,900.00**
(Minus) Down Payment **$ 3,600.00**
Mortgage Loan Amount **$ 68,300.00** × Starting Rate per 1,000 **$ 7.69** = M/P&I* **$ 525.23**
Mortgage L/A **$ 68,300.00** × P.M.I. Premium due at closing **1.25%** = **$ 853.75**
Mortgage L/A **$ 68,300.00** × monthly premium **.40%** = **$ 27.32**

Monthly Payment: (If Mortgage Company Is Using Higher Interest Rate To Qualify Add Difference To Payment)

*Principal and Interest	**$ 525.23**		
¹⁄₁₂ Property Tax	**$ 63.34**	Yearly Property Tax	**$ 760.00**
¹⁄₁₂ Hazard Insurance	**$ 37.09**	Yearly Hazard Insurance	**$ 445.00**
Monthly P.M.I. Premium	**$ 27.32**	Due at Closing P.M.I. Premium	**$ 853.75**
Other	**$ N/A**		
Total Monthly Payment	**$ 652.98**	+ Qualifying Interest Rate Difference if Any	**$ 49.17**
+ Estimated Maintenance	**$ N/A**	is mortgage company counting this	
+ Estimated Utilities	**$ N/A**	is mortgage company counting this	
*Total Monthly Housing Costs	**$ 702.15**	÷ **$ 3,000.00** = 23.40%	

Income net or **gross**   House to Income
*ratio (25)

Monthly Debt:

*Total Monthly Housing Costs	**$ 702.15**
Debt Over (6 Months)	**$ 147.00**
Credit Cards	**$ 47.00**
Child Care	**$ N/A** is mortgage company counting this
Other	**$ N/A**
Total Monthly Debt	**$ 896.15** ÷ **$ 3,000.00** = 29.87%

Income net or **gross**   Debt to Income ratio (33)

Cash Needed To Close:

Down Payment	**$ 3,600.00**	*Pre-Paid Items	
*Pre-Paid Items	**$ 1,998.67**	Hazard Insurance + 2 Months	= **$ 519.18**
If Paying Closing Costs	**$ Seller Paying**	Due at Closing P.M.I. + 2 Months	= **$ 730.82**
Other	**$ N/A**	Taxes #8 of Months?	= **$ 506.72**
Total Cash Needed	**$ 5,598.67**	Interest #15 of Days?	= **$ 241.95**
Do you have cash above this amount?		Total Estimated Pre-Paid Items	**$1,998.67**

EXAMPLE #3
_____

Graduated Payment Mortgage (GPM)

F.H.A.-245 (A) Plan III loan with these specifics:
1) 30 year
2) Fixed rate 10%
3) Payment graduates at 7½% per year for five years
4) Down Payment of 3% for the 1st $25,000, 5% on remainder
5) Discount Points – 4%
6) Qualifying Ratios – 38/53, on net income
7) F.H.A. mortgage insurance premium is 0.038% can be financed in loan
8) Qualify on first year's payment
9) Child Care counted in total debt
10) Estimated Maintenance is $45.00 per month
11) Estimated Utilities is $140.00 per month

Most graduated payment plans have a higher interest rate than a fixed rate mortgage loan. A graduated payment mortgage has some negative amortization. The discount on these loans is usually the same.

A G.E.M. (Growing Equity Mortgage) loan works similarly to a G.P.M. but there is no negative amortization. The loan payments are structured to pay the loan off in a shorter period of time, usually somewhere between eleven and eighteen years.

On the form _How to Figure Down Payment and Yearly Scheduled Payments_ increases, this form can be used for all F.H.A. G.P.M. loans. The factors change with each interest change and on the type G.P.M. plan. So, the factors on payment and down payment would need to be gotten from the mortgage company with the particular G.P.M. plan and interest being used.

Down payments on F.H.A. 245 (A) Plan 3 are figured against percentage factors, but normally require approximately 10% down payment and loans are rounded to the next lowest $50.00 increments.

EXAMPLE #3: Completed Payment Form
F.H.A.

Graduated Payment Mortgage Loan (G.M.P.) Form
Figure Down Payment And Scheduled Payment Increases

Appraised Value Or Sales Price—Whichever Is Less	$ 70,000.00
(Minus) Down Payment	$ 5,700.00
Mortgage Loan Amount	$ 64,300.00

For F.H.A. 245 (A) Plan 3

Sales Price $70,000 × 97 = $67,900 × By Factor%(.9476299) = $64,344
Round To Next Lowest $50.00 $64,300 Max. Loan Amount
Highest Loan Balance Loan Amount $64,300 × Factor%(1.0552642) = Highest
Loan $67,853 (Minus) Loan Amount $64,300 = Deferred Interest $3,533
Loan Amount $64,300 + F.H.A. Mortgage Insurance $2,443 = *$66,743
*Loan Amount

For F.H.A. Mortgage Insurance

Mortgage Loan Amount $64,300.00 × F.H.A. Insurance Due .038% = $ 2,443.40

Scheduled Payment Increases

Year	*Loan Amount	× Factor %	= Monthly Payment
1	$ 66,743.00	× (.0066704)	= $ 445.20
2	$ "	× (.0071706)	= $ 478.59
3	$ "	× (.0077084)	= $ 514.49
4	$ "	× (.0082866)	= $ 553.07
5	$ "	× (.0089081)	= $ 594.55
6	$ "	× (.0095762)	= $ 639.14
7	$ N/A	× (N/A)	= $ "
8	$ N/A	× ( )	= $ "
9	$ N/A	× ( )	= $ "
10	$ N/A	× ( )	= $ "

EXAMPLE #3: Completed Loan Form
F.H.A.
Graduated Payment Mortgage Loans (G.P.M.)
Growing Equity Mortgage Loans (G.E.M.)

Sales Price	$ 70,000.00	Qualification Ratios* 38/53	
(Minus) Down Payment	$ 5,700.00	Interest Rate 10% D. Points 4	
Mortgage Loan Amount	$ 64,300.00	× F.H.A. Insurance Due .038% = $ 2,443.00	
+ F.H.A. Mortgage Insurance	$ 2,443.00		
Total Mortgage Amount	$ 66,743.00		

Yearly Mortgage Payment Increases:

$ 445.20	$ 478.59	$ 514.49	$ 553.07	$ 594.55
First Year	Second Year	Third Year	Fourth Year	Fifth Year
$ 639.14	$ N/A	$ N/A	$ N/A	$ N/A
Sixth Year	Seventh Year	Eighth Year	Ninth Year	Tenth Year

Monthly Payment:

First Year Mo. Payment	$ 445.20		
1/12 Property Tax	$ 63.34	Yearly Property Tax	$ 760.00
1/12 Hazard Insurance	$ 37.09	Yearly Hazard Insurance	$ 445.00
Other	$ N/A		
Total Monthly Payment	$ 545.63		
+ Estimated Maintenance	$ 45.00		
+ Estimated Utilities	$ 140.00		
*Total Monthly Housing Costs	$ 730.63 ÷	$ 2,410.00 =	30.32%

Net Income

or

Gross Income   House to Income *ratio

Monthly Debt:

*Total Monthly Housing Costs	$ 730.63		
Debt Over (6 Months)	$ 147.00		
Credit Cards	$ 47.00		
Child Care	$ 350.00		
Other	$ N/A		
Total Monthly Debt	$ 1,274.63 ÷	$ 2,410.00 =	52.88%

Net Income

or

Gross Income   Debt to Income ratio (53)

Cash Needed To Close:

Down Payment	$ 5,700.00	*Pre-Paid Items	
*Pre-Paid Items	$ 1,280.45	Hazard Insurance + 2 Months	= $ 519.18
Closing Costs?	$ Seller Paying	Taxes #8 of Months?	= $ 506.72
Other	$ .40	Interest #15 of Days?	= $ 254.55
Total Cash Needed	$ 6,980.85	Total Estimated Pre-Paid Items	$1,280.45

Do you have cash above this amount?

EXAMPLE #4   **V.A. insured mortgage loan**

1) Fixed interest rate at 10½%
2) 30 years
3) Discount points – 4
4) Child care
5) Credit cards with balances only, minimum payment
6) Maintenance counted, for this example $40
7) Utilities counted, for this example $135 per month
8) Net income used

V.A. has no present restriction on who can pay closing costs, pre-paid items, or V.A. funding fee. If the veteran is dealing with a willing seller then the seller can pay all costs. The stipulation should read something like this, "Purchaser to pay $1.00 towards closing costs, pre-paid items and V.A. funding fee. Seller to pay balance at time of closing." At present the V.A. funding fee can be financed in with the loan. The mortgage company may require that the $19 of the $719 funding fee be paid in cash, this would make the mortgage amount $72,600, rounding the amount to the nearest fifty dollars.

For this example say the V.A. minimum amount for family support of four people is $733.00 per month. Based on all the examples given this veteran would qualify by income, but there are other considerations such as job stability, credit history.

Based on Debt to Income Ratio, although it is above the 41% limit, if other requirements are met, this loan would probably be approved.

The veteran needs to have good credit and meet all other V.A. requirements.

V.A. Fixed Rate Mortgage Loans

Sales Price	$ 71,900.00	Interest Rate 10½%	D. Points 4
(Minus) Downpayment	$ N/A	If Required	
+ V.A. Funding Fee	$ 719.00		
Mortgage Loan Amount	$ 72,619.00	× rate per 1,000 $ 9.15 = M/P&I*$ 664.46	

Monthly Payment:

*Principal and Interest	$ 664.46		
¹⁄₁₂ Property Tax	$ 63.34	Yearly Property Tax	$ 760.00
¹⁄₁₂ Hazard Insurance	$ 37.09	Yearly Hazard Insurance	$ 445.00
Other	$ N/A		
☆ Total Monthly Payment	$ 764.89		
+ Estimated Maintenance	$ 40.00		
+ Estimated Utilities	$ 135.00		
*Total Monthly Housing Costs	$ 939.89		

Monthly Debt:

*Total Monthly Housing Costs	$ 939.89
☆ Debt Over (6 Months)	$ 147.00
☆ Credit Cards	$ 27.00
☆ Child Care	$ 350.00
Other	$ N/A
Total Monthly Debt	$ 1,463.89

Net Income	$ 2,410.00
*(Minus) Total Debt	$ 1,463.89
Balance	$ 946.11
(Minus) Minimum Amount Required For Family Support	$ 733.00
Balance	$ 213.11

Cash Needed To Close:

Downpayment?	$N/A	*Pre-Paid Items	
*Pre-Paid Items	$ 1.00	Hazard Insurance + 2 Months =	$ Seller Paying
If Paying Closing Costs	$ Seller Paying	Taxes #0 of Months? =	$ Seller Paying
Other	$N/A	Interest #0 of Days? =	$ 1.00
Total Cash Needed	$ 1.00	Total Estimated Pre-Paid Items	$ 1.00

Do you have cash above this amount?

☆ Total Monthly House Payment	$ 764.89
☆ Total Long Term Debt over 6 months	$ 524.00

$1288.89 ÷ $3000.00 = 42.96%

Gross Income   Debt to Income ratio (41)

WHAT'S BEST FOR YOU?

No one rule is cut and dry but there are some general rules of thumb. A fixed rate mortgage loan is best for the family on a budget where the home buyer prefers stability and the knowledge of exactly what he will be paying from year to year. It is also best for the person whose financial position is not going to improve to any great extent over the next few years. However, in a high interest market, the buyer may want to check out the alternatives to the fixed rate mortgage.

An adjustable rate mortgage loan, A.R.M., is especially good for someone who is just getting started and knows that income will increase each year while the loan payments are increasing. The higher the beginning interest rate, the higher the interest rate can go, even with a lifetime cap. An example of this would be a beginning rate of 12 percent with a lifetime cap of 5 percent which could take the interest rate to 17 percent. The A.R.M. loan is a good alternative to the fixed rate mortgage when interest rates are high.

The graduated payment mortgage, G.P.M., is also a good loan for the person who is just getting started. The rule here is to be rather certain that income will continue to increase enough to take care of the increase in payments the first few years. This is definitely not a mortgage for the average buyer in a high interest market. This type loan is best when interest rates are low.

The G.E.M. loan is for the buyer whose income is rather secure. It allows for increased payments in an accelerated period of time so that the mortgage can be paid off quicker. This loan has advantages but it is definitely not for the average home buyer.

Certainly, for the qualified veteran there is no better loan than one that is insured by the Veterans Administration. All the advantages are in the favor and for the benefit of the veteran.

By now, you should have a good idea of just how much interest really costs. Now it is up to you to decide which type loan best suits you. The inner parts of the mortgage loan agreement contribute to the overall loan as well as interest. Each part, like job, family, financial and tax position, is different and this difference will determine the best loan. Should the loan be 15, 20, 25 or 30 years? Should interest be raised to cancel out discount points? What about more downpayment to lower or do away with the P.M.I.? Would a loan assumption be better than a new mortgage loan?

If the buyer does not qualify because of debts perhaps something in cash reserve listing could be sold and used to reduce some of the debt. A particular debt item could be sold to do away with that debt in order to qualify. If the buyer does not qualify for the monthly payments because of income but knows that he would be making more money in a year or so, he could ask the mortgage company about a 3-2-1 or a

2-1 buy down. For example, a 3-2-1 buy down may cost 4 points and a 2-1 buy down may cost 3 points. The interest rate could be raised to do away with the discount points. Then, the discount points could be used for the buy down. In this manner the buyer might qualify for the loan.

Some mortgage companies are not in the habit of carrying on conversations with would be buyers unless they are on contract and are doing business with them. A mortgage company may not spend very much time talking to you on the telephone because they have no idea if your loan will be placed with their company. If this is the attitude, the time may not be beneficial to either of you.

It is far more important to be an informed, knowledgeable mortgage buyer, no matter what company is being used, than it is for you to try to choose your own mortgage company. The mortgage representative will respect the fact that you have attempted to find out all that you could concerning the mortgage loan market and he is likely to secure for you the best loan possible within his company. So many buyers have no idea what is best for them that they take the advice of others and accept whatever is offered to them in the way of a mortgage loan program.

Anyone can keep up with current interest rate. It is not difficult to find out what rate is being offered. It is important to be sure that the quotes you hear are not artificially low using a seller buy down. You need to know the "true" interest rate. This way you will know what is a realistic interest quote, one that you can use as an indicator for what you can expect to get.

Therefore, when you find the house that you like you will know if the seller's sources are good or if you should seek another mortgage source. Builders and real estate companies sometimes offer buy downs on their homes. They may reduce the price by the cost of the buy down and this may be better for you.

FORMS

On the next few pages are some forms that may help you obtain the information you need to see how you will qualify for a loan. You will not need the information on each type loan, only the ones that may be best for you. You may not need all the information on one form, at one time, perhaps only enough to see how you like the way the loan is working out or how one company's specifics compare to another. Since interest and/or points are subject to change daily, you will need to compare mortgage companies on the same day. Otherwise the information may not be comparable.

These forms are not meant to be a complete list of everything a person needs to know about the loans. They are only a guide. Review the other chapters in determining what other information may be pertinent to a particular loan.

If for some reason you do not qualify for the type loan or amount you would like, when you use these forms, do not hesitate to call a mortgage company and have them go over the information with you. They may be able to tell you what options are open to you on the current market. The important thing for you to know is what is best for you, not only in interest rate but also in the inner workings of the loan agreement.

QUESTIONS TO ASK MORTGAGE COMPANY
On **Conventional Fixed Rate** Mortgage Loans

Loans To Value Available   95% ☐   90% ☐   Other _____

Interest Rate _____%   Discount Points _____   Loan Origination Fee _____%

Any Limits On Seller Contributions _____   If So What Do You Count As Seller Contributions _____

Do You Have Buy Downs — Costs On 3-2-1 _____   2-1 _____   Other _____

Can Interest Be Increased To Remove Discount Points

If So Interest Rate _____

P.M.I. Due At Closing   95% _____%   90% _____%   Other _____%
P.M.I. Monthly Premium   95% _____%   90% _____%   Other _____%
Any Other P.M.I. Payment Plan   95% _____%   90% _____%   Other _____%

Approximate Charges For Closing Costs

Amount $_____   Or _____%   Of Loan Amount

Any Other Charges — Document Fees, Photo, etc. _____

If I Sell This House Is The Loan:

Assumable ☐   Non Qualifying ☐   Or   Qualifying ☐

Non Escalating ☐   Or   Escalating ☐   If So Amount $_____ Or _____%

Prepayment Penalty   No ☐   Yes ☐   If So Amount $_____ Or _____%

Any Other Features In This Loan _____

Qualification Ratios _____/_____

Housing Costs Figured Against   Net Income ☐   Or   Gross Income ☐

What Makes Up Housing Costs:

Principal And Interest ☐   Monthly P.M.I. Premium ☐   Property Tax ☐

Hazard Insurance ☐   Estimated Maintenance ☐   If So Costs Used _____

Estimated Utilities ☐   If So Costs Used _____   Association Fee ☐

Other _____

What Counts As Debt:

A Debt 10 Months Or Less Is It Counted ☐   6 Months Or Less Counted ☐

Or Other _____

How Are Credit Cards Viewed _____

Child Care Count As Debt _____

Life Insurance Count As Debt _____

Car Insurance Count As Debt _____

Anything Else That Would Count As Debt _____

Approximately How Long Does It Take To Get A Loan Approved _____

Do You Have Anything Better In A Fixed Rate Loan — State, County, City Or Other _____

Conventional Fixed Rate Mortgage Loans
95% – 90% – Other L.T.V. (loan to value)

Sales Price $_____   Qualification Ratios*_____ / _____

(Minus) Downpayment $_____ Interest Rate _____%   D. Points _____

Mortgage Loan Amount $_____ × rate per 1,000 $_____ = M/P&I* $_____

Mortgage L/A $_____ × P.M.I. Premium due at closing _____% = $_____

Mortgage L/A $_____ × P.M.I. monthly premium _____% = $_____

Monthly Payment:

* Principal And Interest $_____

1/12 Property Tax $_____   Yearly Property Tax $_____

1/12 Hazard Insurance $_____   Yearly Hazard Insurance $_____

Monthly P.M.I. Premium $_____   Due at Closing P.M.I. Premium $_____

Other $_____

Total Monthly Payment $_____

+ Estimated Maintenance $_____   is mortgage company counting this

+ Estimated Utilities $_____   is mortgage company counting this

* Total Monthly Housing Costs $_____ ÷ $_____   = _____%

                           income net or gross   House to Income

                                      *ratio (   )

Monthly Debt:

* Total Monthly Housing Costs $_____

Debt Over (_____ Months) $_____

Credit Cards $_____

Child Care $_____   is mortgage company counting this

Other $_____

Total Monthly Debt $_____ ÷ $_____   = _____%

                           income net or gross   Debt to Income ratio (   )

Cash Needed To Close:

Downpayment $_____   *Pre-Paid Items

* Pre-Paid Items $_____   Hazard Insurance + 2 Months = $_____

If Paying Closing Costs $_____   Due at Closing P.M.I. + 2 Months = $_____

Other $_____   Taxes #_____ of Months? = $_____

Total Cash Needed $_____   Interest #_____ of Days? = $_____

Do you have cash above this amount?   Total Estimated Pre-Paid Items $_____

QUESTIONS TO ASK MORTGAGE COMPANY
On **F.H.A. Fixed Rate** Mortgage Loans

Maximum Loan To Value Available* _____

Downpayment _____

Interest Rate _____%   Discount Points _____   Loan Origination Fee _____%

F.H.A. Mortgage Insurance Due _____%

Any Limits On Seller Contributions _____   If So What Do You Count As Seller Contributions _____

Do You Have Buy Downs—Costs On 3-2-1 _____   2-1 _____   Other _____

Can Interest Be Increased To Remove Discount Points

If So Interest Rate _____

Approximate Charges For Closing Costs

Amount $_____   Or _____% Of Loan Amount

Any Other Charges—Document Fees, Photo, etc. _____

Qualification Ratios _____/_____ Net Income ☐   Gross Income ☐

Estimated Maintenance Costs Used _____

Estimated Utilities Costs Used _____

Any Other _____

What Counts As Debt:

A Debt 10 Months Or Less Is It Counted ☐   6 Months Or Less Counted ☐

Or Other _____

How Are Credit Cards Viewed _____

Child Care Count As Debt _____

Life Insurance Count As Debt _____

Car Insurance Count As Debt _____

Anything Else That Would Count As Debt_____

Approximately How Long Does It Take To Get A Loan Approved _____

Is Your Company F.H.A. Delegated _____

Do You Have Anything Better In A Fixed Rate Loan—State, County, City Or Other _____

---

*F.H.A. At Present Will Add And Finance Closing Costs And Mortgage Insurance Premium In With The Mortgage Loan As Long As It Does Not Exceed Their Maximum Loan Amount

F.H.A. Fixed Rate Mortgage Loans

Sales Price + Closing Costs $_____   Qualification Ratios*   _____/_____

(Minus) Downpayment $_____   Interest Rate _____%   D. Points _____

Mortgage Loan Amount $_____ × F.H.A. Insurance Due _____% = $_____

+ F.H.A. Mortgage Insurance $_____

Total Mortgage Amount $_____ × rate per 1,000 $_____ = M/P&I* $_____

Monthly Payment:

* Principal And Interest $_____

$\frac{1}{12}$ Property Tax $_____   Yearly Property Tax $_____

$\frac{1}{12}$ Hazard Insurance $_____   Yearly Hazard Insurance $_____

Other $_____

Total Monthly Payment $_____

+ Estimated Maintenance $_____

+ Estimated Utilities $_____

* Total Monthly Housing Costs $_____ ÷ $_____ = _____%

         Net Income   House to Income
         or   *Ratio ( )
         Gross Income

Monthly Debt:

* Total Monthly Housing Costs $_____

Debt Over (_____ Months) $_____

Credit Cards $_____

Child Care $_____

Other $_____

Total Monthly Debt $_____ ÷ $_____ = _____%

         Net Income   Debt to Income ratio ( )
         or
         Gross Income

Cash Needed To Close:

Downpayment $_____   *Pre-Paid Items

* Pre-Paid Items $_____   Hazard Insurance + 2 Months = $_____

Closing Costs? $_____   Taxes #_____ of Months? = $_____

Other $_____   Interest #_____ of Days? = $_____

Total Cash Needed $_____   Total Estimated Pre-Paid Items $_____

Do you have cash above this amount?

QUESTIONS TO ASK MORTGAGE COMPANY
On **V.A. Fixed Rate** Mortgage Loans

Maximum Loan Available _____

Any Downpayment Required _____

Interest Rate _____%   Discount Points _____   Loan Origination Fee _____%

V.A. Funding Fee _____%

Do You Have Buy Downs

Costs On 3-2-1 _____   2-1 _____   Other _____

Can Interest Be Increased To Remove Discount Points

If So Interest Rate _____

Approximate Charges For Closing Costs:

Amount $_____   Or _____% Of Loan Amount

Any Other Charges—Document Fees, Photos, etc. _____

What Counts As Debt:

A Debt 10 Months Or Less Is It Counted ☐   6 Months Or Less Counted ☐

Or Other _____

How Are Credit Cards Viewed _____

Child Care Counted As Debt _____

Life Insurance Counted As Debt _____

Car Insurance Counted As Debt _____

Estimated Maintenance Costs Used _____

Estimated Utilities Costs Used _____

Anything Else That Would Count As Debt_____

Approximately How Long Does It Take To Get A Loan Approved _____

Is Your Company V.A. Automatic _____

Do You Have Anything Better In A Fixed Rate Loan—State, County, City Or Other _____

_____

How Much Money Is Required After All Monthly Housing Costs And Debt To Be Left For Family Support _____

Income Ratio, What Counts As Total Monthly House Payment? _____

_____

What Counts As Debts?_____

_____

Computed, Is This Ratio On Net Or Gross Income? _____

May Want To Get Information On V.A. Graduated Payment Mortgage Loan (G.M.P.)

V.A. Fixed Rate Mortgage Loans

Sales Price $_____   Interest Rate _____%   D. Points _____

(Minus) Downpayment $_____   If Required

+ V.A. Funding Fee $_____

Mortgage Loan Amount $_____ × rate per 1,000 $_____ = M/P&I* $_____

Monthly Payment:

* Principal And Interest $_____
1/12 Property Tax $_____   Yearly Property Tax $_____
1/12 Hazard Insurance $_____   Yearly Hazard Insurance $_____
Other $_____
☆ Total Monthly Payment $_____
+ Estimated Maintenance $_____
+ Estimated Utilities $_____
* Total Monthly Housing Costs $_____

Monthly Debt:

* Total Monthly Housing Costs $_____
☆ Debt Over (____ Months) $_____
☆ Credit Cards $_____
☆ Child Care $_____
Other $_____
Total Monthly Debt $_____

Net Income $_____
* (Minus) Total Debt $_____
Balance $_____
(Minus) Minimum Amount Required For Family Support $_____
Balance $_____

Cash Needed To Close:

Downpayment? $_____   *Pre-Paid Items
* Pre-Paid Items $_____   Hazard Insurance + 2 Months = $_____
If Paying Closing Costs $_____   Taxes #_____ of Months? = $_____
Other $_____   Interest #_____ of Days? = $_____
Total Cash Needed $_____   Total Estimated Pre-Paid Items $_____
Do you have cash above this amount?

☆ Total Monthly House Payment $_____
☆ Total Long Term Debt over 6 months $_____

$_____ ÷ $_____ = $_____
gross income   Debt to Income
ratio ( )

QUESTIONS TO ASK MORTGAGE COMPANY
On Conventional Adjustable Rate Mortgage Loans (A.R.M.)

Loans To Value Available   95% ☐   90% ☐   Other _____

Starting Interest Rate _____%   Discount Points _____

Loan Origination Fee _____%

Is Accruing Interest Rate The Same Interest Rate _____

What Is Loan Indexed To _____   Index Rate Now _____%

Do You Have Highest _____% (Rate) And Lowest _____% (Rate) Of Index

Last 5 Years   What Is The Margin Rate _____%

How Often Does This Loan Adjust (New Payment)_____

Does This Loan Have Adjustment Interest Cap _____% Or Is It A

Payment Cap _____%   Does This Loan Have Lifetime Interest Caps _____%

Does This Loan Have Any Negative Amortization _____

Any Limits On Seller Contributions _____ If So What Counts As Seller Contributions _____

Do You Have Buy Downs—Costs On 3-2-1 _____   2-1 _____   Other _____

Can Interest Be Increased To Remove Discount Points   If So Interest Rate _____

P.M.I. Due At Closing   95% _____%   90% _____%   Other _____%

P.M.I. Monthly Premium   95% _____%   90% _____%   Other _____%

Any Other P.M.I. Payment Plan   95% _____%   90% _____%   Other _____%

Approximate Charges For Closing Costs

Amount $_____   Or _____%   Of Loan Amount

Any Other Charges—Document Fees, Photo, etc. _____

If I Sell This House Is The Loan:

Assumable ☐   Non Qualifying ☐   Or   Qualifying ☐

Non Escalating ☐   Or   Escalating ☐   If So Amount $_____ Or _____%

Prepayment Penalty   No ☐   Yes ☐   If So Amount $_____ Or _____%

Does Loan Have A Convertible Feature To Lock In A Fixed Interest Rate At A Later Date _____

If So Costs _____

Any Other Features In This Loan _____

Qualification Ratios _____ / _____

Housing Costs Figured Against   Net Income ☐   Or   Gross Income ☐

What Makes Up Housing Costs:

Principal And Interest ☐   Monthly P.M.I. Premium ☐   Property Tax ☐

Hazard Insurance ☐   Estimated Maintenance ☐   If So Costs Used _____

Estimated Utilities ☐   If So Costs Used _____   Association Fee ☐

Other_____

What Counts As Debt:

A Debt 10 Months Or Less Is It Counted ☐   6 Months Or Less Counted ☐   Or Other _____

How Are Credit Cards Viewed _____

Child Care Count As Debt _____

Life Insurance Count As Debt _____

Car Insurance Count As Debt _____

Anything Else That Would Count As Debt_____

Approximately How Long Does It Take To Get A Loan Approved _____

Do You Have Anything Better In A Mortgage Loan—State, County, City Or Other _____

Conventional
Adjustable Rate Mortgage Loans (A.R.M.)
95% – 90% – Other L.T.V. (loan to value)

Index Rate Now _____%   Qualification Ratios* _____/_____

Margin _____%   Starting Interest Rate _____%   D. Points _____

Total _____%   Is This A Higher Rate Than Starting Interest Rate

Yearly Interest Cap _____%   Life Of Loan Interest Cap _____% + _____% = _____%

Starting Rate   Highest Rate

Sales Price $_____
(Minus) Downpayment $_____
Mortgage Loan Amount $_____ × S.I. rate per 1,000 $_____ = M/P&I* $_____
Mortgage L/A $_____ × P.M.I. Premium due at closing _____% = $_____
Mortgage L/A $_____ × P.M.I. monthly premium _____% = $_____

Monthly Payment: (If Mortgage Company Is Using Higher Interest
*Principal And Interest $_____   Rate To Qualify Add Difference To Payment)
1/12 Property Tax $_____   Yearly Property Tax $_____
1/12 Hazard Insurance $_____   Yearly Hazard Insurance $_____
Monthly P.M.I. Premium $_____   Due at Closing P.M.I. Premium $_____
Other $_____
Total Monthly Payment $_____ + Qualifying Interest Rate Difference if Any $_____
+ Estimated Maintenance $_____ is mortgage company counting this
+ Estimated Utilities $_____ is mortgage company counting this
*Total Monthly Housing Costs $_____ ÷ $_____ = _____%

income net or gross   House to Income
*ratio (   )

Monthly Debt:
*Total Monthly Housing Costs $_____
Debt Over (_____ Months) $_____
Credit Cards $_____
Child Care $_____   is mortgage company counting this
Other $_____
Total Monthly Debt $_____ ÷ $_____ = _____%

income net or gross   Debt to Income ratio (   )

Cash Needed To Close:
Downpayment $_____   *Pre-Paid Items
*Pre-Paid Items $_____   Hazard Insurance + 2 Months = $_____
If Paying Closing Costs $_____   Due at Closing P.M.I. + 2 Months = $_____
Other $_____   Taxes #_____ of Months? = $_____
Total Cash Needed $_____   Interest #_____ of Days? = $_____
Do you have cash above this amount?   Total Estimated Pre-Paid Items $_____

QUESTIONS TO ASK MORTGAGE COMPANY
On F.H.A. Adjustable Rate Mortgage Loans (A.R.M.)

Maximum Loan To Value Available* _____

Downpayment _____

Starting Interest Rate _____%   Discount Points _____

Loan Origination Fee _____%   F.H.A. Mortgage Insurance Due _____%

What Is Loan Indexed To _____ Index Rate Now _____%

Do You Have Highest _____% (Rate) And Lowest _____% (Rate) Of Index

Last 5 Years   What Is The Margin Rate _____%

How Often Does This Loan Adjust (New Payment) _____

Adjustment Interest Cap _____%   Lifetime Interest Caps _____%

Any Limits On Seller Contributions _____ If So What Do You Count As Seller Contributions _____

Do You Have Buy Downs—Costs On 3-2-1 _____ 2-1 _____ Other _____

Can Interest Be Increased To Remove Discount Points

If So Interest Rate _____

Approximate Charges For Closing Costs:

Amount $_____ Or _____% Of Loan Amount

Any Other Charges—Document Fees, Photo, etc. _____

Does Loan Have A Convertible Feature To Lock In A Fixed Interest Rate

At A Later Date _____ If So Costs _____

Any Other Features In This Loan _____

Qualification Ratios _____/_____ Net Income ☐ Gross Income ☐

Estimated Maintenance Costs Used _____

Estimated Utilities Costs Used _____

Any Other _____

What Counts As Debt:

A Debt 10 Months Or Less Is It Counted ☐   6 Months Or Less Counted ☐

Or Other _____

How Are Credit Cards Viewed _____

Child Care Count As Debt _____

Life Insurance Count As Debt _____

Car Insurance Count As Debt _____

Anything Else That Would Count As Debt _____

Approximately How Long Does It Take To Get A Loan Approved _____

Is Your Company F.H.A. Delegated _____

Do You Have Anything Better In A Mortgage Loan—State, County, City Or Other _____

---

*F.H.A. At Present Will Add And Finance Closing Costs And Mortgage Insurance Premium In With The Mortgage Loan As Long As It Does Not Exceed Their Maximum Loan Amount

F.H.A.
Adjustable Rate Mortgage Loans (A.R.M.)

Index Rate Now   _____%   Qualification Ratios * _____/_____

Margin   _____%   Starting Interest Rate _____%   D. Points _____

Total   _____%   Is This A Higher Rate Than Starting Interest Rate

Yearly Interest Cap _____%   Life Of Loan Interest Cap _____% + _____% = _____%

                                                             Starting Rate   Highest Rate

Sales Price + Closing Costs $_____

(Minus) Downpayment $_____

Mortgage Loan Amount $_____ × F.H.A. Insurance Due _____% = $_____

+ F.H.A. Mortgage Insurance $_____

Total Mortgage Amount $_____ × S.I. rate per 1,000 $_____ = M / P & I * $_____

Monthly Payment: (If Mortgage Company Is Using Higher Interest

* Principal And Interest $_____   Rate To Qualify Add Difference To Payment)

1/12 Property Tax $_____   Yearly Property Tax $_____

1/12 Hazard Insurance $_____   Yearly Hazard Insurance $_____

Other $_____

Total Monthly Payment $_____ + Qualifying Interest Rate Difference if Any $_____

+ Estimated Maintenance $_____

+ Estimated Utilities $_____

* Total Monthly Housing Costs $_____ ÷ $_____ = _____%

                                Net Income   House to Income

                                   or   * ratio (   )

                                Gross Income

Monthly Debt:

* Total Monthly Housing Costs $_____

Debt Over (_____ Months) $_____

Credit Cards $_____

Child Care $_____

Other $_____

Total Monthly Debt $_____ ÷ $_____ = _____%

                                Net Income   Debt to Income ratio (   )

                                   or

                                Gross Income

Cash Needed To Close:

Downpayment $_____   * Pre-Paid Items

* Pre-Paid Items $_____   Hazard Insurance + 2 Months = $_____

Closing Costs? $_____   Taxes #_____ of Months? = $_____

Other $_____   Interest #_____ of Days? = $_____

Total Cash Needed $_____   Total Estimated Pre-Paid Items $_____

Do you have cash above this amount?

QUESTIONS TO ASK MORTGAGE COMPANY
On **Conventional Graduated Payment** Mortgage Loans (G.M.P.)

Loans To Value Available   95% ☐   90% ☐   Other _____
Or Downpayment Factor _____
Interest Rate _____%   Discount Points _____   Loan Origination Fee _____%
Any Limits On Seller Contributions _____   If So What Do You Count As Seller Contributions _____
Do You Have Buy Downs—Costs On 3-2-1 _____   2-1 _____   Other _____
Can Interest Be Increased To Remove Discount Points   If So Interest Rate _____

P.M.I. Due At Closing   95% _____%   90% _____%   Other _____%
P.M.I. Monthly Premium   95% _____%   90% _____%   Other _____%
Any Other P.M.I. Payment Plan 95% _____%   90% _____%   Other _____%

Percent Payments Can Increase Each Year _____%
Yearly Mortgage Payment Increases Or Factors:

$_____ $_____ $_____ $_____ $_____
First Year   Second Year   Third Year   Fourth Year   Fifth Year
$_____ $_____ $_____ $_____ $_____
Sixth Year   Seventh Year   Eighth Year   Ninth Year   Tenth Year
Highest Loan Balance Will Get $_____ Or Factor _____

Approximate Charges For Closing Costs
Amount $_____   Or _____% Of Loan Amount
Any Other Charges—Document Fees, Photo, etc. _____

If I Sell This House Is The Loan:
Assumable ☐   Non Qualifying ☐   Or   Qualifying ☐
Non Escalating ☐   Or   Escalating ☐   If So Amount $_____ Or _____%
Prepayment Penalty   No ☐   Yes ☐   If So Amount $_____ Or _____%
Any Other Features In This Loan _____

Qualification Ratios _____ / _____
Housing Costs Figured Against   Net Income ☐   Or   Gross Income ☐
What Makes Up Housing Costs:
Principal And Interest ☐   Monthly P.M.I. Premium ☐   Property Tax ☐
Hazard Insurance ☐   Estimated Maintenance ☐   If So Costs Used _____
Estimated Utilities ☐   If So Costs Used _____   Association Fee ☐
Other_____

What Counts As Debt:
A Debt 10 Months Or Less Is It Counted ☐   6 Months Or Less Counted ☐   Or Other _____
How Are Credit Cards Viewed _____
Child Care Count As Debt _____
Life Insurance Count As Debt _____
Car Insurance Count As Debt _____
Anything Else That Would Count As Debt_____
Approximately How Long Does It Take To Get A Loan Approved _____
Do You Have Anything Better In A Mortgage Loan—State, County, City Or Other _____

Conventional
Graduated Payment Mortgage Loan (G.M.P.) Form:
Figure Downpayment And Scheduled Payment Increases

Appraised Value Or Sales Price—Whichever Is Less $_____

(Minus) Downpayment $_____

Mortgage Loan Amount $_____

% (L.T.V.) Used For Downpayment

Loan To Value (L.T.V.) _____% × (sales Price) $_____ = $_____ (Loan Amount)

Round To Next Lowest $50.00 = *$_____ Max. Loan Amount

Highest Loan Balance   Loan Amount $_____ × Factor % (   ) = Highest

Loan $_____ (Minus) Loan Amount $_____ = Deferred Interest $_____

% (L.T.V.) Used To Highest Loan Balance For Downpayment

(sales Price) $_____ × _____% Loan To Value (L.T.V.) = $_____ (Loan

Amount) ÷ By Factor % (   ) = $_____ Round To Next Lowest $50.00 =

*$_____ Max. Loan Amount

Highest Loan Balance   Loan Amount $_____ × Factor % (   ) = Highest

Loan $_____ (Minus) Loan Amount $_____ = Deferred Interest $_____

Scheduled Payment Increases

Year	*Loan Amount ×	Factor%	= Monthly P&I Payment
1	$_____	× ( )	= $_____
2	$_____	× ( )	= $_____
3	$_____	× ( )	= $_____
4	$_____	× ( )	= $_____
5	$_____	× ( )	= $_____
6	$_____	× ( )	= $_____
7	$_____	× ( )	= $_____
8	$_____	× ( )	= $_____
9	$_____	× ( )	= $_____
10	$_____	× ( )	= $_____

Conventional
Graduated Payment Mortgage Loans (G.P.M.)
Growing Equity Mortgage Loan (G.E.M.)

Sales Price $_____   Qualification Ratios *_____/_____

(Minus) Downpayment $_____   Interest Rate _____%   D. Points _____

Mortgage Loan Amount $_____

Mortgage L/A $_____ × P.M.I. Premium due at closing _____% = $_____

Mortgage L/A $_____ × P.M.I. monthly premium _____% = $_____

Yearly Mortgage Payment Increases:

$_____	$_____	$_____	$_____	$_____
First Year	Second Year	Third Year	Fourth Year	Fifth Year
$_____	$_____	$_____	$_____	$_____
Sixth Year	Seventh Year	Eighth Year	Ninth Year	Tenth Year

Monthly Payment:

First Year Monthly Payment $_____

$\frac{1}{12}$ Property Tax $_____   Yearly Property Tax $_____

$\frac{1}{12}$ Hazard Insurance $_____   Yearly Hazard Insurance $_____

Monthly P.M.I. Premium $_____   Due at Closing P.M.I. Premium $_____

Other $_____

Total Monthly Payment $_____

+ Estimated Maintenance $_____   is mortgage company counting this

+ Estimated Utilities $_____   is mortgage company counting this

* Total Monthly Housing Costs $_____ ÷ $_____ = _____%

     income net or gross   House to Income

       * ratio ( )

Monthly Debt:

* Total Monthly Housing Costs $_____

Debt Over (_____ Months) $_____

Credit Cards $_____

Child Care $_____   is mortgage company counting this

Other $_____

Total Monthly Debt $_____ ÷ $_____ = _____%

     income net or gross   Debt to Income ratio ( )

Cash Needed To Close:

Downpayment $_____   * Pre-Paid Items

* Pre-Paid Items $_____   Hazard Insurance + 2 Months = $_____

If Paying Closing Costs $_____   Due at Closing P.M.I. + 2 Months = $_____

Other $_____   Taxes #_____ of Months? = $_____

Total Cash Needed $_____   Interest #_____ of Days? = $_____

Do you have cash above this amount?   Total Estimated Pre-Paid Items $_____

QUESTIONS TO ASK MORTGAGE COMPANY
On F.H.A. Graduated Payment Mortgage Loans (G.M.P.)

Type Mortgage Loan Plan _____

Maximum Loan To Value Available* _____

Downpayment Factor_____

Interest Rate _____%   Discount Points _____   Loan Origination Fee _____%

F.H.A. Mortgage Insurance Due _____%

Any Limits On Seller Contributions _____   If So What Do You Count As Seller Contributions _____

Can Interest Be Increased To Remove Discount Points

If So Interest Rate _____

Percent Payments Can Increase Each Year _____%

Yearly Mortgage Payment Increases Or Factors:

$_____	$_____	$_____	$_____	$_____
First Year	Second Year	Third Year	Fourth Year	Fifth Year
$_____	$_____	$_____	$_____	$_____
Sixth Year	Seventh Year	Eighth Year	Ninth Year	Tenth Year

Highest Loan Balance Will Get $_____ Or Factor _____

Approximate Charges For Closing Costs

Amount $_____   Or _____%   Of Loan Amount

Any Other Charges—Document Fees, Photo, etc. _____

Qualification Ratios _____/_____   Net Income ☐   Gross Income ☐

Estimated Maintenance Costs Used _____

Estimated Utilities Costs Used _____

Any Other _____

What Counts As Debt:

A Debt 10 Months Or Less Is It Counted ☐   6 Months Or Less Counted ☐

Or Other _____

How Are Credit Cards Viewed _____

Child Care Count As Debt _____

Life Insurance Count As Debt _____

Car Insurance Count As Debt _____

Anything Else That Would Count As Debt_____

Approximately How Long Does It Take To Get A Loan Approved _____

Is Your Company F.H.A. Delegated _____

Do You Have Anything Better In A Mortgage Loan—State, County, City Or Other _____

---

*F.H.A. At Present Will Add And Finance Closing Costs And Mortgage Insurance Premiums In With The Mortgage Loan As Long As It Does Not Exceed Their Maximum Loan Amount

F.H.A.
Graduated Payment Mortgage Loan (G.M.P.) Form:
Figure Downpayment And Scheduled Payment Increases

Appraised Value Or Sales Price—Whichever Is Less $_____

(Minus) Downpayment $_____

Mortgage Loan Amount $_____

For F.H.A. 245(A) Plan _____

Sales Price $_____ × 97 = $_____ ÷ Factor% (   ) = $_____

Rounded To Next Lowest $50.00 $_____ Max Loan Amount

Highest Loan Balance   Loan Amount $_____ × Factor % (   ) = Highest

Loan $_____ (Minus) Loan Amount $_____ = Deferred Interest $_____

Loan Amount $_____ + F.H.A. Mortgage Insurance $_____ = *$_____

*Loan Amount

For F.H.A. Mortgage Insurance

Mortgage Loan Amount $_____ × F.H.A. Insurance Due _____% = $_____

Scheduled Payment Increases

Year	*Loan Amount ×	Factor%	= Monthly Payment
1	$_____	×( )	= $_____
2	$_____	×( )	= $_____
3	$_____	×( )	= $_____
4	$_____	×( )	= $_____
5	$_____	×( )	= $_____
6	$_____	×( )	= $_____
7	$_____	×( )	= $_____
8	$_____	×( )	= $_____
9	$_____	×( )	= $_____
10	$_____	×( )	= $_____

F.H.A.
Graduated Payment Mortgage Loans (G.P.M.)
Growing Equity Mortgage Loans (G.E.M.)

Sales Price + Closing Costs $_____   Qualification Ratios *_____ / _____

(Minus) Downpayment $_____   Interest Rate _____%   D. Points _____

Mortgage Loan Amount $_____ × F.H.A. Insurance Due _____% = $_____

+ F.H.A. Mortgage Insurance $_____

Total Mortgage Amount $_____

Yearly Mortgage Payment Increases:

$_____	$_____	$_____	$_____	$_____
First Year	Second Year	Third Year	Fourth Year	Fifth Year
$_____	$_____	$_____	$_____	$_____
Sixth Year	Seventh Year	Eighth Year	Ninth Year	Tenth Year

Monthly Payment:

First Year Mo. Payment $_____

$\frac{1}{12}$ Property Tax $_____   Yearly Property Tax $_____

$\frac{1}{12}$ Hazard Insurance $_____   Yearly Hazard Insurance $_____

Other $_____

Total Monthly Payment $_____

+ Estimated Maintenance $_____

+ Estimated Utilities $_____

* Total Monthly Housing Costs $_____ ÷ $_____ = _____ %

         Net Income   House to Income

           or   *ratio (   )

        Gross Income

Monthly Debt:

* Total Monthly Housing Costs $_____

Debt Over (_____ Months) $_____

Credit Cards $_____

Child Care $_____

Other $_____

Total Monthly Debt $_____ ÷ $_____ = _____ %

         Net Income   Debt to Income ratio (   )

           or

        Gross Income

Cash Needed To Close:

Downpayment $_____   *Pre-Paid Items

*Pre-Paid Items $_____   Hazard Insurance + 2 Months = $_____

Closing Costs? $_____   Taxes #_____ of Months? = $_____

Other $_____   Interest #_____ of Days? = $_____

Total Cash Needed $_____   Total Estimated Pre-Paid Items $_____

Do you have cash above this amount?

13

How to Spot the Investor Trap

There are a number of seminars and books on the market that teach how anyone can "Buy a House for Nothing Down." Basically, what they are selling is the idea of how to make it big or get rich quick in real estate. Some of the methods taught are inventive ways of alternate types of financing. The problem is that, sometimes, these methods lack integrity and not everything is above the table. For example, it is being taught that when writing a contract the seller should always have a "weasel" clause, a way out of the deal using such phrases as "subject to partner's approval" when in fact there is no partner. If with one breath these folks are teaching deceit, how can a person believe the rest of what is being said? The ear of greed hears what it wants to hear.

THE FORECLOSURE TRAP

Some books will teach you to watch the legal paper for the foreclosures and try to get the house by paying the back payments and any legal fees. Is taking advantage of the buyer or seller getting the best deal or is it another thing altogether? The idea that once a house has been bought at a marvelously low price, it can be resold for a fantastic profit just isn't true, in the vast majority of cases. Some of these alternative methods of financing being taught are not readily accepted in the marketplace.

The real question that needs to be addressed and answered is how do you safeguard yourself from someone who has just enough knowledge, from one of these sessions or books, to get both of you in trouble. There are no free rides. You can pay now or later. Unfortunately, you can also pay now and later, in the too good to be true deals.

Most of us have heard that if you eat carrots you will have good eyesight, because you don't see rabbits wearing glasses. For the moment

THE CARROT THEORY

try to change the way you see things, as you begin to spot the investor trap. Things, very often, are not what they seem.

Rather than accepting the fact that carrots give rabbits good eyesight, let's say that actually they make the rabbits' ears grow long. An investor/seller buys houses and resells them. He is not usually an owner/occupant. He will not usually sell with a new loan. In other words, he lets someone assume an old loan. The fact is that a new loan would require that the house be appraised and this limits his profit and ability to wheel and deal.

The seller/investor is limited to a degree by the original recorded mortgage loan agreement. He can rent with option, use shared equity, sell with little or nothing down with a second mortgage or allow buyer to take over payments with little or nothing down. All these creative ways to own a home can be legal, but the buyer should beware because the seller/investor can make a bad deal look good. There are some questions to ask to investigate these alternatives. These questions should help you evaluate the validity of the deal.

When rent with option to buy is offered, who sets the sale price? Is this price a fair market value for the house?

On a shared equity purchase if the downpayment is one or two thousand dollars this may mean that the seller will recoup most if not all of his investment with your downpayment. In a shared equity agreement the price for the house and the percent of ownership are usually set by the investor/seller. This should be by agreement of the parties. It is possible that the seller could get most, if not all, of his money out of the house and still own 50% or more of the house, while the buyer made all the payments. And at the same time the seller could have 50% of the taxes written off in his behalf. This is a great deal for the seller but what kind of deal is it for the buyer?

The investor/seller may be willing to sell the house for $500.00 to $2,000 downpayment and, for any difference owing, he would take a second mortgage. The question here is who set the price of the house; is the second mortgage actually the seller's additional profit? The buyer may be paying through the nose to get into this house for $500 down. Time might show that the buyer would have been far better off to have waited and saved than to have been entangled in a web of additional homeowner debts. An investor will not tie up very much of his own money because he would not have the funds to continue to do business. The object of the investor is to be in and out of a deal as quickly as possible with as little cash as possible used in the process.

The second mortgage that the seller has gotten from the buyer can be sold. At a discount, it will bring between 50 to 75 cents per dollar depending upon the yield and the number of years of the second mortgage.

The investor does not have to wait any number of years to realize a profit.

Next, the seller/investor is willing for the buyer to take over payments with only a small downpayment, somewhere between $500 and $1,000. Now, the would-be home buyer says "That is a fantastic deal!" Although on the surface that appears to be the case, the next few paragraphs will explain that the actual situation may be just the opposite.

1) For $500 downpayment the buyer takes over the first and second mortgage payments. The first mortgage payment is made to a mortgage company. Who gets the second mortgage payment? Perhaps it is made out to his wife or his corporation, maybe to him or to a bank. The second mortgage may have just been placed on the house. He may sell the second mortgage immediately after your purchase.

None of this will affect your payment. There is nothing wrong with this. It is important, however, that you understand that you are not really buying this house for the downpayment. There is more behind the scenes, knowledge of which this book attempts to make you fully aware.

2) If the house has only one mortgage payment, is this payment made out to an individual? There is a possibility that this situation is a *wrap around mortgage*. In a wrap around mortgage the payments may go from one company or individual to another before they get to the original mortgage holder. Wrap around mortgages may not be used on some mortgage loan agreements. A wrap around mortgage can be placed on a house regardless of the number of mortgages already on it. The wrap around can be at any interest rate, any amount of money, and any number of years regardless of the value of the house.

3) The house could be sold for little or nothing down with a *land contract*. In a land contract the buyer only keeps possession as long as he makes the payments on the land contract, not a mortgage. The holder of the land contract still keeps title to the property and the buyer has only an equitable interest in the house.

Buying a house for little or nothing down can be a good deal but the key is to know what houses are selling for in the area. You can always overpay; you seldom will underpay. If the agreement is—or appears to be—one-sided, chances are it is not a good deal.

THE BIGGER FOOL THEORY

Although some claim this to be so, it just isn't true that no matter what price a person pays for property, he can always sell it to someone else for more. This myth comes into play primarily when someone tries to "wheel and deal" with little or no knowledge of the real estate market. A person going to one of the "get rich quick" real estate seminars may get taken by another investor who is just ahead of the game.

This more experienced investor may sell his property to the novice investor, letting him have it—in more ways than one.

After having gotten this great deal on an investment house, the novice investor is off to sell it at a profit, only to find that there are no takers. In other words, there are no bigger fools left. Whoever has the house at this time must wait for someone even more foolish to arrive on the scene. Don't let that one be you.

QUESTIONS TO ASK

There are almost always some good deals available, but there are bad ones, too. If you don't know the values in the area and don't ask the right questions you could be victimized by one of the bad deals. Not everyone is out to get you, so don't let paranoia set in. However, a word to the wise is appropriate. Sometimes, not knowingly, people take advantage of each other. Most will try to help whenever possible; it is the exception that you need to watch out for. And you cannot afford even one exception. Ask the questions and do the research. Here are the "homework" assignments.

1) Ask if the house has been appraised. If so, when and by which lending company. Ask if you may see a copy of the appraisal. If the house has not been appraised, that is all the more reason for you to know the values in the neighborhood. If the appraisal is over a year old and the house has been for sale for that long, it may be overpriced. If there is an appraisal, is the appraising company willing to make a loan to a buyer at that appraised price? If there is an appraisal but the seller will not let you see it, you should act as though no appraisal has been made. Loan assumptions do not need appraisals in most cases. You don't need an appraisal to determine if the price is fair: you don't, that is, if you have done your "homework."

2) If the property is renting with an option to buy, what is the value of the house? What are the agreements of the sale? You want to be sure that the rent and sale price are in line.

3) If shared equity is the offer, once again you need to know the value and understand completely the agreements of the sale. You will get nothing for nothing. Be sure that you don't give something for nothing. In other words don't agree to a ridiculous one-sided sale. It is (mostly) your money. Ask what the loan balance is on the original mortgage and what the age of that mortgage is. How long has the seller owned the house? If the loan balance is considerably lower than the asking price, the house is probably overpriced. This would be especially true if the house has just been purchased. If a mortgage has been placed on the house very recently, what kind of mortgage is it? If the seller has just purchased the house it is even more important for you to know what you are doing and to ask questions. The seller may not

own the house but, rather, just have a contract and you may be the partner he was talking about in his weasel clause.

4) If there is a second mortgage you will need to ask how long it has been in effect. Also you should ask to whom is the second mortgage paid? How long has the current seller owned the house? Is the mortgage paid to a company or an individual? Think about it this way: if the house has just been purchased, is the seller, out of the goodness of his heart, going to re-sell it for nothing? This will help you judge the fairness of the deal. You should know if you are dealing with an owner/occupant or seller/investor.

5) Ask the question, "Is this mortgage a wrap around or a land contract?" If so, you should talk with an attorney or real estate broker before going any further. Seeking professional advice on deals of this type is the very best thing to do. Did you know that with a wrap around mortgage you could pay your payment and your house could still go into foreclosure if the party to whom you made your payment failed to pass the payment on to the original mortgage holder? With a land contract you have no mortgage, only a contract.

Be careful. Be thorough. Be deliberate. You should always know the value of similar houses in the area and the condition of the house you are thinking about buying. You need to know and understand every part of the sales contract and loan agreement being offered. If you are not 100% sure then you should ask more questions. When in doubt, seek professional help. Every type loan agreement can serve a useful purpose. Just be sure it is your purpose that is being served.

Summary

In the mortgage market, rules, requirement guidelines, interest rates and points keep changing. It would be virtually impossible to give precise information about these items alone, much less on a specific mortgage loan. The specifics probably would be out of date before the book was printed. This book offers information and the know-how to apply it. With these tools the informed buyer can decide for himself what loan is best. When you are preparing to buy a home, you owe it to yourself to be an informed consumer. This book has been written to help you, the prospective homebuyer, become just that.

The investor looks for security, low risk, good return or yield, and liquidity on his investments. You should adopt the attitude of the investor and be on the lookout for these very same things. After all, this probably is the biggest investment of your life.

One reason some of the requirements in the mortgage market keep changing is that efforts are made to resolve problems. There are better ways to qualify buyers, better ways to lend money to builders for construction. The problem seems to be that lending institutions are slow to change. In our opinion, there are two sure ways to bring about change: through education, which is the first purpose of this book, and through need, which, not coincidentally, is the second reason for this book.

Much thought, concern, and consideration has gone into the writing of this book. It is our hope that it will help you arrange a mortgage loan that will be exactly right for your needs, and that the loan provides you and your family with the home of your dreams.

Index